The
PUFFIN BOOK *of*
CLASSIC VERSE

The
PUFFIN BOOK *of*
CLASSIC VERSE

EDITED BY

Raymond Wilson

ILLUSTRATED BY

Diz Wallis

VIKING

ACKNOWLEDGEMENT

With special thanks to
Susan Dickinson for her
editorial guidance

VIKING

Published by the Penguin Group
Penguin Books Ltd, 27 Wrights Lane, London W8 5TZ, England
Penguin Books USA Inc., 375 Hudson Street, New York, New York 10014, USA
Penguin Books Australia Ltd, Ringwood, Victoria, Australia
Penguin Books Canada Ltd, 10 Alcorn Avenue, Toronto, Ontario, Canada M4V 3B2
Penguin Books (NZ) Ltd, 182–190 Wairau Road, Auckland 10, New Zealand

Penguin Books Ltd, Registered Offices: Harmondsworth, Middlesex, England

This collection first published 1995
1 3 5 7 9 10 8 6 4 2

This collection copyright © Raymond Wilson, 1995
Illustrations copyright © Diz Wallis, 1995

The Acknowledgements on page 383 constitute an extension of this copyright page

Typeset by Datix International Ltd, Bungay, Suffolk
Filmset in Monophoto Garamond 14/16

Made and printed in Great Britain by Clays Ltd, St Ives plc
A CIP catalogue record for this book is available from the British Library
ISBN 0-670-85312-7

Contents

CREATURES

VERY REMARKABLE BEASTS   95

GHOSTS, GHOULS AND WITCHES 107

THE SEA 117

SONG AND DANCE   187

PEOPLE   209

FIGURES OF FUN   233

SCHOOL   247

THE CITY

WAR

REFLECTIONS 295

SEASONS 309

JOURNEY'S END   341

Acknowledgements   383

INTRODUCTION

For a poem to be classic, it must be the best of its kind, but even a glance at this anthology will make you realize that, in form alone, there are many different kinds of poem: epics, sonnets, lyrics, ballads, limericks. But there is, too, an enormous range in the subject matter of poetry, and this variety is reflected in the different sections of this anthology, which groups poems under such headings as Creatures, or People, or Love, or War, or the Seasons.

What I have tried to ensure is that all the poems chosen should, in their different ways, add to our appreciation of life. Many of the poems rouse in us a sense of wonder by revealing a magic that lies just below the surface of things – even everyday and commonplace things. Such poems teach us, as William Blake says:

> To see a world in a grain of sand,
> And a heaven in a wild flower.

But there are poems here, too, which can set us laughing at curious people and remarkable beasts; there are supernatural poems that can set our nerves on edge; there are poems to set us dreaming and poems to set our feet dancing.

As an anthologist, I have tried to achieve a number of things: to introduce you to what is often called the heritage of English poetry; to celebrate the richness and variety of this heritage, and to group and set side by side poems in a way that invites you to make comparisons and notice contrasts. The word anthology originally meant a collection of flowers, and if poems can be likened to flowers, there's all the difference in the world between their being carefully arranged in a vase and their being stuffed indiscriminately into a pot!

Of the several aims I set myself, the most important aim was never to forget what Dryden calls 'the chief end' of poetry, which is the giving of delight. This, above all, is the true purpose of this anthology. I hope you will find as great a pleasure in reading it as I have done in compiling it.

Raymond Wilson

1995

COME! COME AWAY!

Away! Away!

A way, away from men and towns,
To the wild wood and the downs –
To the silent wilderness.
Where the soul need not repress
Its music, lest it should not find
An echo in another's mind . . .

from The Invitation, Percy Bysshe Shelley

Tony O

O ver the bleak and barren snow
A voice there came a-calling;
'Where are you going to, Tony O!
Where are you going this morning?'

'I am going where there are rivers of wine,
The mountains bread and honey;
There Kings and Queens do mind the swine,
And the poor have all the money.'

Anonymous

When I Set Out for Lyonnesse

When I set out for Lyonnesse,
    A hundred miles away,
    The rime was on the spray,
And starlight lit my lonesomeness
When I set out for Lyonnesse
    A hundred miles away.

What should bechance at Lyonnesse
    While I should sojourn there
    No prophet durst declare,
Nor did the wisest wizard guess
What would bechance at Lyonnesse
    While I should sojourn there.

When I came back from Lyonnesse
    With magic in my eyes,
    All marked with mute surmise
My radiance rare and fathomless,
When I came back from Lyonnesse
    With magic in my eyes!

Thomas Hardy

When Green Buds Hang

When green buds hang in the elm like dust
    And sprinkle the lime like rain,
Forth I wander, forth I must,
    And drink of life again.
Forth I must by hedgerow bowers
    To look at the leaves uncurled,
And stand in the fields where cuckoo-flowers
    Are lying about the world.

                    A. E. Housman

A Great Time

Sweet Chance, that led my steps abroad,
    Beyond the town, where wild flowers grow –
A rainbow and a cuckoo, Lord,
    How rich and great the times are now!
        Know, all ye sheep
        And cows, that keep
On staring that I stand so long
    In grass that's wet from heavy rain –
A rainbow and a cuckoo's song
    May never come together again;
        May never come
        This side the tomb.

                    W. H. Davies

A Boy's Song

Where the pools are bright and deep,
Where the grey trout lies asleep,
Up the river and over the lea,
That's the way for Billy and me.

Where the blackbird sings the latest,
Where the hawthorn blooms the sweetest,
Where the nestlings chirp and flee,
That's the way for Billy and me.

Where the mowers mow the cleanest,
Where the hay lies thick and greenest,
There to track the homeward bee,
That's the way for Billy and me.

Where the hazel bank is steepest,
Where the shadow falls the deepest,
Where the clustering nuts fall free,
That's the way for Billy and me.

This I know, I love to play,
Through the meadow, among the hay,
Up the water and over the lea,
That's the way for Billy and me.

James Hogg

THE LAKE ISLE OF INNISFREE

I will arise and go now, and go to Innisfree,
And a small cabin build there, of clay and wattles made:
Nine bean rows will I have there, a hive for the honey-bee,
   And live alone in the bee-loud glade.

And I shall have some peace there, for peace comes dropping
   slow,
Dropping from the veils of the morning to where the cricket
   sings;
There midnight's all a glimmer, and noon a purple glow,
   And evening full of the linnet's wings.

I will arise and go now, for always night and day
I hear lake water lapping with low sounds by the shore;
While I stand on the roadway, or on the pavements grey,
   I hear it in the deep heart's core.

William Butler Yeats

THE VAGABOND

Give to me the life I love,
Let the lave go by me,
Give the jolly heaven above
And the by-way nigh me.
Bed in the bush with stars to see,
Bread I dip in the river –
There's the life for a man like me,
There's the life for ever.

Let the blow fall soon or late,
Let what will be o'er me;
Give the face of earth around
And the road before me.
Wealth I seek not, hope nor love,
Nor a friend to know me;
All I seek, the heaven above
And the road below me.

Or let the autumn fall on me
Where afield I linger,
Silencing the bird on tree,
Biting the blue finger.
White as meal the frosty field –
Warm the fireside haven –
Not to autumn will I yield,
Not to winter even!

Let the blow fall soon or late,
Let what will be o'er me;
Give the face of earth around,
And the road before me.
Wealth I ask not, hope nor love,
Nor a friend to know me.
All I ask, the heaven above,
And the road below me.

Robert Louis Stevenson

My Heart's in the Highlands

My heart's in the Highlands, my heart is not here;
My heart's in the Highlands a-chasing the deer;
Chasing the wild deer, and following the roe;
My heart's in the Highlands, wherever I go.
Farewell to the Highlands, farewell to the North,
The birthplace of valour, the country of worth;
Wherever I wander, wherever I rove,
The hills of the Highlands for ever I love.

Farewell to the mountains, high-covered with snow;
Farewell to the straths and green valleys below;
Farewell to the forests and wild-hanging woods;
Farewell to the torrents and loud-pouring floods.
My heart's in the Highlands, my heart is not here;
My heart's in the Highlands a-chasing the deer;
Chasing the wild deer, and following the roe;
My heart's in the Highlands, wherever I go.

Robert Burns

LEISURE

What is this life if, full of care,
We have no time to stand and stare?

No time to stand beneath the boughs
And stare as long as sheep or cows.

No time to see, when woods we pass,
Where squirrels hide their nuts in grass.

No time to see, in broad daylight,
Streams full of stars, like skies at night.

No time to turn at Beauty's glance,
And watch her feet, how they can dance.

No time to wait till her mouth can
Enrich that smile her eyes began.

A poor life this if, full of care,
We have no time to stand and stare.

W. H. Davies

THE ROAD NOT TAKEN

Two roads diverged in a yellow wood,
And sorry I could not travel both
And be one traveller, long I stood
And looked down one as far as I could
To where it bent in the undergrowth;

Then took the other, as just as fair,
And having perhaps the better claim,
Because it was grassy and wanted wear;
Though as for that the passing there
Had worn them really about the same,

And both that morning equally lay
In leaves no step had trodden black.
Oh, I kept the first for another day!
Yet knowing how way leads on to way,
I doubted if I should ever come back.

I shall be telling this with a sigh
Somewhere ages and ages hence:
Two roads diverged in a wood, and I –
I took the one less travelled by,
And that has made all the difference.

                                    Robert Frost

THE GOLDEN ROAD

HASSAN
  Sweet to ride forth at evening from the wells,
      When shadows pass gigantic on the sand,
  And softly through the silence beat the bells
      Along the Golden Road to Samarkand.

ISHAK
  We travel not for trafficking alone;
      By hotter winds our fiery hearts are fanned:
  For lust of knowing what should not be known
      We take the Golden Road to Samarkand.

MASTER OF THE CARAVAN
  Open the gate, O watchman of the night!

THE WATCHMAN
      Ho, travellers, I open. For what land
  Leave you the dim-moon city of delight?

MERCHANTS (*with a shout*)
      We take the Golden Road to Samarkand!

              (*The Caravan passes through the gate*)
THE WATCHMAN (*consoling the women*)
  What would ye, ladies? It was ever thus.
      Men are unwise and curiously planned.

A WOMAN
  They have their dreams, and do not think of us.

VOICES OF THE CARAVAN (*in the distance singing*)
  We take the Golden Road to Samarkand.

                              James Elroy Flecker

O TO SAIL

O to sail in a ship,
To leave this steady unendurable land,
To leave the tiresome sameness of the streets, the sidewalks
and the houses,
To leave you, O you solid motionless land, and entering a
ship,
To sail and sail and sail!

Walt Whitman

BABYLON

'How many miles to Babylon?'
'Three-score and ten.'
'Can I get there by candle-light?'
'Yes, and back again.'

If your heels are nimble and light,
You may get there by candle-light.

Anonymous

To Sail Beyond the Sunset

Come, my friends,
'Tis not too late to seek a newer world.
Push off, and sitting well in order smite
The sounding furrows; for my purpose holds
To sail beyond the sunset, and the baths
Of all the western stars, until I die.
It may be that the gulfs will wash us down:
It may be we shall touch the Happy Isles,
And see the great Achilles, whom we knew.
Tho' much is taken, much abides; and tho'
We are not now that strength which in old days
Moved earth and heaven; that which we are, we are;
One equal temper of heroic hearts,
Made weak by time and fate, but strong in will
To strive, to seek, to find, and not to yield.

from Ulysses, Alfred, Lord Tennyson

ALL IN A DAY

HAPPY THE MAN

Happy the man, and happy he alone,
   He who can call today his own;
He who, secure within, can say,
   Tomorrow, do thy worst, for I have lived today.

                      John Dryden

COCK-CROW

Out of the wood of thoughts that grows by night
To be cut down by the sharp axe of light, –
Out of the night, two cocks together crow,
Cleaving the darkness with a silver blow:
And bright before my eyes twin trumpeters stand,
Heralds of splendour, one at either hand,
Each facing each as in a coat of arms:
The milkers lace their boots up at the farms.

                    Edward Thomas

HARK, HARK! THE LARK

Hark, hark! The lark at heaven's gate sings
   And Phoebus 'gins arise,
His steeds to water at those springs
   On chaliced flowers that lies;
And winking mary-buds begin
   To ope their golden eyes;
With everything that pretty is,
   My lady, sweet, arise!
     Arise, arise!

from Cymbeline, William Shakespeare

SISTER, AWAKE

Sister, awake! close not your eyes.
  The day her light discloses,
And the bright morning doth arise
  Out of her bed of roses.

See the clear sun, the world's bright eye,
  In at our window peeping:
Lo, how he blusheth to espy
  Us idle wenches sleeping!

Therefore awake! make haste, I say,
  And let us, without staying,
All in our gowns of green so gay
  Into the park a-maying.

                              Anonymous

UP IN THE MORNING

Up in the morning's no for me,
  Up in the morning early;
When a' the hills are covered wi' snaw,
  I'm sure it's winter fairly.

Cauld blaws the wind frae east to west,
  The drift is driving sairly;
Sae loud and shrill I hear the blast,
  I'm sure it's winter sairly.

Up in the morning's no for me,
  Up in the morning early;
When a' the hills are covered wi' snaw,
  I'm sure it's winter fairly.

The birds sit chittering in the thorn,
  A' day they fare but sparely;
And long's the night frae even to morn,
  I'm sure it's winter fairly.

Up in the morning's no for me,
  Up in the morning early;
When a' the hills are covered wi' snaw,
  I'm sure it's winter fairly.

Robert Burns

MORNING AFTER A STORM

*T*here was a roaring in the wind all night;
The rain came heavily and fell in floods;
But now the sun is rising calm and bright;
The birds are singing in the distant woods;
Over his own sweet voice the stock-dove broods;
The Jay makes answer as the Magpie chatters;
And all the air is filled with pleasant noise of waters.

All things that love the sun are out of doors;
The sky rejoices in the morning's birth;
The grass is bright with rain-drops – on the moors
The hare is running races in her mirth;
And with her feet she from the plashy earth
Raises a mist, that, glittering in the sun,
Runs with her all the way, wherever she doth run.

William Wordsworth

NOON

The midday hour of twelve the clock counts o'er,
    A sultry stillness lulls the air asleep;
The very buzz of flies is heard no more,
    Nor faintest wrinkles o'er the waters creep.
Like one large sheet of glass the pool does shine,
    Reflecting in its face the burnt sunbeam:
The very fish their sturting play decline,
    Seeking the willow shadows 'side the stream.
And, where the hawthorn branches o'er the pool,
    The little bird, forsaking song and nest,
Flutters on dripping twigs his limbs to cool,
    And splashes in the stream his burning breast.
Oh, free from thunder, for a sudden shower,
To cherish nature in this noonday hour!

John Clare

In a Cornfield

A silence of full noontide heat
Grew on them at their toil:
The farmer's dog woke up from sleep,
The green snake hid her coil
Where grass grew thickest; bird and beast
Sought shadows as they could,
The reaping men and women paused
And sat down where they stood;
They ate and drank and were refreshed,
For rest from toil is good.

Christina Rossetti

Days

*W*hat are days for?
Days are where we live.
They come, they wake us
Time and time over.
They are to be happy in:
Where can we live but days?

Ah, solving that question
Brings the priest and the doctor
In their long coats
Running over the fields.

Philip Larkin

from SUMMER EVENING

Crows crowd croaking overhead,
Hastening to the woods to bed.
Cooing sits the lonely dove,
Calling home her absent love.
With 'Kirchup! Kirchup!' 'mong the wheats,
Partridge distant partridge greets . . .

Bats flit by in hood and cowl;
Through the barn-hole pops the owl;
From the hedge, in drowsy hum,
Heedless buzzing beetles bum,
Haunting every bushy place,
Flopping in the labourer's face . . .

John Clare

SUNSET

The summer sun is sinking low;
Only the tree-tops redden and glow;
Only the weather-cock on the spire
Of the village church is a flame of fire;
All is in shadow below.

Henry Wadsworth Longfellow

Hymn to Diana

Queen and huntress, chaste and fair,
    Now the sun is laid to sleep,
Seated in thy silver chair,
    State in wonted manner keep:
        Hesperus entreats thy light,
        Goddess excellently bright.

Earth, let not thy envious shade
    Dare itself to interpose;
Cynthia's shining orb was made
    Heaven to clear when day did close;
        Bless us then with wishèd sight,
        Goddess excellently bright.

Lay thy bow of pearl apart,
    And thy crystal-shining quiver;
Give unto the flying hart
    Space to breathe, how short soever:
        Thou that mak'st a day of night,
        Goddess excellently bright.

Ben Jonson

MIDNIGHT

. . . *M*idnight was come, when every vital thing
With sweet sound sleep their weary limbs did rest,
The beasts were still, the little birds that sing
Now sweetly slept, beside their mother's breast,
The old and all were shrouded in their nest:
 The waters calm, the cruel seas did cease,
 The woods, and fields, and all things held their peace.

The golden stars were whirled amid their race,
And on the earth did laugh with twinkling light,
When each thing, nestled in his resting place,
Forgat day's pain with pleasure of the night:
The hare had not the greedy hounds in sight,
 The fearful deer of death stood not in doubt,
 The partridge dreamed not of the falcon's foot.

The ugly bear now minded not the stake,
Nor how the cruel mastives do him tear;
The stag lay still unrousèd from the brake;
The foamy boar feared not the hunter's spear:
All things were still, in desert, bush, and brere:
 With quiet heart, now from their travails ceased,
 Soundly they slept in midst of all their rest.

Thomas Sackville

brere: briar, brushwood

A Good-Night

Close now thine eyes, and rest secure;
  Thy soul is safe enough, thy body sure;
  He that loves thee, he that keeps
And guards thee, never slumbers, never sleeps . . .

Francis Quarles

from Dream-Pedlary

If there were dreams to sell,
      What would you buy?
Some cost a passing bell;
      Some a light sigh,
That shakes from Life's fresh crown
Only a rose-leaf down.
If there were dreams to sell,
Merry and sad to tell,
And the crier rang the bell,
      What would you buy?

Thomas Lovell Beddoes

CREATURES

I Think I Could Turn and Live with Animals

I think I could turn and live with animals, they're so
  placid and self-contained,
I stand and look at them long and long.

They do not sweat and whine about their condition,
They do not lie awake in the dark and weep for their sins,
They do not make me sick discussing their duty to God,
Not one is dissatisfied, not one is demented with the
  mania of owning things,
Not one kneels to another, nor to his kind that lived
  thousands of years ago,
Not one is respectable or unhappy over the whole earth.

Walt Whitman

My Cat Jeoffry

For I will consider my cat Jeoffry.
For he is the servant of the Living God, duly and daily
    serving him . . .
For first he looks upon his fore-paws to see if they are
    clean.
For secondly he kicks up behind to clear away there.
For thirdly he works it upon stretch with the fore-paws
    extended.
For fourthly he sharpens his paws by wood.
For fifthly he washes himself.
For sixthly he rolls upon wash.
For seventhly he fleas himself, that he may not be
    interrupted upon the beat.
For eighthly he rubs himself against a post.
For ninthly he looks up for his instructions.
For tenthly he goes in quest of food.
For having considered God and himself he will consider
    his neighbour
For if he meets another cat he will kiss her in kindness.
For when he takes his prey he plays with it to give it chance.
For one mouse in seven escapes by his dallying.
For when his day's work is done his business more
    properly begins.
For he keeps the Lord's watch in the night against the
    adversary.

For he counteracts the powers of darkness by his electrical
  skin and glaring eyes.
For he counteracts the Devil, who is death, by brisking
  about the life.
For in his morning orisons he loves the sun and the sun
  loves him.
For he is of the tribe of Tiger.
For the Cherub Cat is a term of the Angel Tiger.
For he has the subtlety and hissing of a serpent, which in
  goodness he suppresses.
For he will not do destruction if he is well-fed, neither will
  he spit without provocation.
For he purrs in thankfulness, when God tells him he's a
  good Cat.

Christopher Smart

THE TOM-CAT

At midnight in the alley
   A Tom-cat comes to wail,
And he chants the hate of a million years
   As he swings his snaky tail.

Malevolent, bony, brindled,
   Tiger and devil and bard,
His eyes are coals from the middle of Hell
   And his heart is black and hard.

He twists and crouches and capers
   And bares his curved sharp claws,
And he sings to the stars of the jungle nights,
   Ere cities were, or laws.

Beast from a world primeval,
   He and his leaping clan,
When the blotched red moon leers over the roofs
   Give voice to their scorn of man.

He will lie on a rug to-morrow
   And lick his silky fur,
And veil the brute in his yellow eyes
   And play he's tame, and purr.

But at midnight in the alley
   He will crouch again and wail,
And beat the time for his demon's song
   With a swing of his demon's tail.

                              Don Marquis

Take One Home for the Kiddies

On shallow straw, in shadeless glass,
Huddled by empty bowls, they sleep:
No dark, no dam, no earth, no grass –
Mam, get us one of them to keep.

Living toys are something novel,
But it soon wears off somehow.
Fetch the shoebox, fetch the shovel –
Mam, we're playing funerals now.

Philip Larkin

SHEEP

When I was once in Baltimore,
    A man came up to me and cried,
'Come, I have eighteen hundred sheep,
    And we will sail on Tuesday's tide.

'If you will sail with me, young man,
    I'll pay you fifty shillings down;
These eighteen hundred sheep I take
    From Baltimore to Glasgow town.'

He paid me fifty shillings down,
    I sailed with eighteen hundred sheep;
We soon had cleared the harbour's mouth,
    We soon were in the salt sea deep.

The first night we were out at sea
    Those sheep were quiet in their mind;
The second night they cried with fear –
    They smelt no pastures in the wind.

They sniffed, poor things, for their green fields,
    They cried so loud I could not sleep:
For fifty thousand shillings down
    I would not sail again with sheep.

W. H. Davies

SHEEP IN WINTER

*T*he sheep get up and make their many tracks
And bear a load of snow upon their backs,
And gnaw the frozen turnip to the ground
With sharp quick bite, and then go noising round
The boy that pecks the turnips all the day
And knocks his hands to keep the cold away
And laps his legs in straw to keep them warm
And hides behind the hedges from the storm.
The sheep, as tame as dogs, go where he goes
And try to shake their fleeces from the snows,
Then leave their frozen meal and wander round
The stubble stack that stands beside the ground,
And lie all night and face the drizzling storm
And shun the hovel where they might be warm.

John Clare

THE WOODMAN'S DOG

Shaggy, and lean, and shrewd, with pointed ears,
And tail cropped short, half lurcher and half cur –
His dog attends him. Close behind his heel
Now creeps he slow; and now, with many a frisk
Wide-scampering, snatches up the drifted snow
With ivory teeth, or ploughs it with his snout;
Then shakes his powdered coat, and barks for joy.

William Cowper

Coyote

*B*lown out of the prairie in twilight and dew,
Half bold and half timid, yet lazy all through;
Loth ever to leave, and yet fearful to stay,
He limps in the clearing, – an outcast in grey.

A shade on the stubble, a ghost by the wall,
Now leaping, now limping, now risking a fall,
Lop-eared and large-jointed, but ever alway
A thoroughly vagabond outcast in grey.

Here, Carlo, old fellow, he's one of your kind, –
Go seek him, and bring him in out of the wind.
What! snarling, my Carlo! So – even dogs may
Deny their own kin in the outcast in grey.

Well, take what you will, – though it be on the sly,
Marauding or begging, – I shall not ask why;
But will call it a dole, just to help on his way
A four-footed friar in orders of grey!

Bret Harte

from THE NYMPH COMPLAINING FOR THE DEATH OF HER FAWN

The wanton troopers riding by
Have shot my fawn, and it will die.
Ungentle men! They cannot thrive
To kill thee. Thou ne'er didst, alive,
Them any harm; alas, nor could
Thy death yet do them any good . . .

It is a wondrous thing how fleet
'Twas on those little silver feet;
With what a pretty skipping grace
It oft would challenge me the race;
And, when't had left me far away,
'Twould stay, and run again, and stay;
For it was nimbler much than hinds,
And trod as if on the four winds.

Andrew Marvell

THE FALLOW DEER AT THE LONELY HOUSE

One without looks in to-night
    Through the curtain-chink
From the sheet of glistening white;
One without looks in to-night
    As we sit and think
    By the fender-brink.

We do not discern those eyes
    Watching in the snow;
Lit by lamps of rosy dyes
We do not discern those eyes
    Wondering, aglow,
    Fourfooted, tiptoe.

Thomas Hardy

THE DONKEY

When fishes flew and forests walked
    And figs grew upon thorn,
Some moment when the moon was blood
    Then surely I was born;

With monstrous head and sickening cry
    And ears like errant wings,
The devil's walking parody
    On all four-footed things.

The tattered outlaw of the earth,
    Of ancient crooked will:
Starve, scourge, deride me: I am dumb,
    I keep my secret still.

Fools! For I also had my hour;
    One far fierce hour and sweet:
There was a shout about my ears,
    And palms before my feet.

G. K. Chesterton

The Runaway

Once when the snow of the year was beginning to fall,
We stopped by a mountain pasture to say, 'Whose colt?'
A little Morgan had one forefoot on the wall,
The other curled at his breast. He dipped his head
And snorted at us. And then he had to bolt.
We heard the miniature thunder where he fled,
And we saw him, or thought we saw him, dim and grey,
Like a shadow against the curtain of falling flakes.
'I think the little fellow's afraid of the snow.
He isn't winter-broken. It isn't play
With the little fellow at all. He's running away.
I doubt if even his mother could tell him, "Sakes,
It's only weather." He'd think she didn't know!
Where is his mother? He can't be out alone.'
And now he comes again with clatter of stone,
And mounts the wall again with whited eyes
And all his tail that isn't hair up straight.
He shudders his coat as if to throw off flies.
'Whoever it is that leaves him out so late,
When other creatures have gone to stall and bin,
Ought to be told to come and take him in.'

Robert Frost

THE FLOWER-FED BUFFALOES

The flower-fed buffaloes of the spring
In the days of long ago,
Ranged where the locomotives sing
And the prairie flowers lie low: —
The tossing, blooming, perfumed grass
Is swept away by the wheat,
Wheels and wheels and wheels spin by
In the spring that still is sweet.
But the flower-fed buffaloes of the spring
Left us, long ago.
They gore no more, they bellow no more,
They trundle around the hills no more: —
With the Blackfeet, lying low,
With the Pawnees, lying low,
Lying low.

Vachel Lindsay

The Tyger

*T*yger! Tyger! burning bright
In the forests of the night,
What immortal hand or eye
Could frame thy fearful symmetry?

In what distant deeps or skies
Burnt the fire of thine eyes?
On what wings dare he aspire?
What the hand dare seize the fire?

And what shoulder, and what art,
Could twist the sinews of thy heart?
And when thy heart began to beat,
What dread hand? and what dread feet?

What the hammer? what the chain?
In what furnace was thy brain?
What the anvil? what dread grasp
Dare its deadly terrors clasp?

When the stars threw down their spears,
And watered heaven with their tears,
Did he smile his work to see?
Did he who made the Lamb make thee?

Tyger! Tyger! burning bright
In the forests of the night,
What immortal hand or eye,
Dare frame thy fearful symmetry?

William Blake

Two Performing Elephants

He stands with his forefeet on the drum
and the other, the old one, the pallid hoary female
must creep her great bulk beneath the bridge of him.

On her knees, in utmost caution
all agog, and curling up her trunk
she edges through without upsetting him.
Triumph! the ancient, pig-tailed monster!

When her trick is to climb over him
with what shadow-like slow carefulness
she skims him, sensitive
as shadows from the ages gone and perished
in touching him, and planting her round feet.

While the wispy, modern children, half-afraid
watch silent. The looming of the hoary, far-gone ages
is too much for them.

                                        D. H. Lawrence

Sweet Suffolk Owl

Sweet Suffolk Owl, so trimly dight
With feathers, like a lady bright,
Thou sing'st alone, sitting by night,
      Te whit! Te whoo! Te whit! To whit!

Thy note that forth so freely rolls
With shrill command the mouse controls;
And sings a dirge for dying souls –
      Te whit! Te whoo! Te whit! To whit!

Thomas Vautor

dight: dressed

THE DEAD SPARROW

*T*ell me not of joy; there's none,
Now my little Sparrow's gone:
    He, just as you,
    Would try and woo,
He would chirp and flatter me;
He would hang the wing awhile –
Till at length he saw me smile
Lord, how sullen he would be!

He would catch a crumb, and then
Sporting, let it go agen;
    He from my lip
    Would moisture sip;
He would from my trencher feed;
Then would hop, and then would run,
And cry *Philip* when he'd done.
O! whose heart can choose but bleed?

O how eager would he fight,
And ne'er hurt, though he did bite.
    No morn did pass,
    But on my glass
He would sit, and mark and do
What I did – now ruffle all
His feathers o'er, now let 'em fall;
And then straightway sleek them too.

Whence will Cupid get his darts
Feathered now to pierce our hearts?
     A wound he may
     Not, Love, convey,
Now this faithful bird is gone;
  O let mournful turtles join
  With loving red-breasts, and combine
To sing dirges o'er his stone!

           William Cartwright

A Bird Came Down the Walk

A bird came down the walk.
He did not know I saw.
He bit an angleworm in halves
And ate the fellow raw,

And then he drank a dew
From a convenient grass,
And then hopped sidewise to the wall
To let a beetle pass.

He glanced with rapid eyes
That hurried all around;
They looked like frightened beads, I thought;
He stirred his velvet head

Like one in danger, cautious;
I offered him a crumb,
And he unrolled his feathers
And rode him softer home

Than oars divide the ocean,
Too silver for a seam,
Or butterflies off banks of noon
Leap, plashless as they swim.

Emily Dickinson

The Twa Corbies

As I was walking all alane,
I heard twa corbies making a mane:
The tane unto the tither did say,
'Whar sall we gang and dine the day?'

'– In behind yon auld fail dyke
I wot there lies a new-slain knight;
And naebody kens that he lies there
But his hawk, his hound, and his lady fair.

'His hound is to the hunting gane,
His hawk to fetch the wild-fowl hame,
His lady's ta'en anither mate,
So we may mak' our dinner sweet.

'Ye'll sit on his white hause-bane,
And I'll pick out his bonny blue e'en:
Wi' ae lock o' his gowden hair
We'll theek our nest when it grows bare.

'Mony a one for him maks mane,
But nane sall ken whar he is gane:
O'er his white banes, when they are bare,
The wind sall blaw for evermair.'

Anonymous

corbies: ravens
fail dyke: turf ditch
theek: thatch

PHEASANT

You said you would kill it this morning.
Do not kill it. It startles me still,
The jut of that odd, dark head, pacing

Through the uncut grass on the elm's hill.
It is something to own a pheasant,
Or just to be visited at all.

I am not mystical: it isn't
As if I thought it had a spirit.
It is simply in its element.

That gives it a kingliness, a right.
The print of its big foot last winter,
The tail-track, on the snow in our court –

The wonder of it, in that pallor,
Through crosshatch of sparrow and starling.
Is it its rareness, then? It is rare.

But a dozen would be worth having,
A hundred, on that hill – green and red,
Crossing and recrossing: a fine thing!

It is such a good shape, so vivid.
It's a little cornucopia.
It unclaps, brown as a leaf, and loud,

Settles in the elm, and is easy.
It was sunning in the narcissi.
I trespass stupidly. Let be, let be.

Sylvia Plath

THAMES GULLS

*B*eautiful it is to see
On London Bridge the bold-eyed seabirds wheel,
And hear them cry, and all for a light-flung crust
Fling us their wealth, their freedom, speed and gleam.
        And beautiful to see
Them that pass by lured by these birds to stay,
And smile and say 'how tame they are' – how tame!
Friendly as stars to steersmen in mid seas,
And as remote as midnight's darling stars,
Pleasant as voices heard from days long done,
As nigh the hand as windflowers in the woods,
And inaccessible as Dido's phantom.

Edmund Blunden

Two Swans

With that, I saw two swans of goodly hue
Come softly swimming down along the lee;
Two fairer birds I yet did never see;
The snow which doth the top of Pindus strew
Did never whiter shew,
Nor Jove himself, when he a swan would be
For love of Leda, whiter did appear;
Yet Leda was, they say, as white as he,
Yet not so white as these, nor nothing near;
So purely white they were,
That even the gentle stream, the which them bare,
Seemed foul to them, and bade his billows spare
To wet their silken feathers, lest they might
Soil their fair plumes with water not so fair,
And mar their beauties bright,
That shone as heaven's light
Against their bridal day, which was not long:
    Sweet Thames, run softly, till I end my song.

from Prothalamion, Edmund Spenser

The Eagle

*H*e clasps the crag with crooked hands;
   Close to the sun in lonely lands,
Ringed with the azure world, he stands.

The wrinkled sea beneath him crawls;
He watches from his mountain walls,
And like a thunderbolt he falls.

          Alfred, Lord Tennyson

HUMMING-BIRD

I can imagine, in some other world
Primeval-dumb, far back
In that most awful stillness, that only gasped and
    hummed,
Humming-birds raced down the avenues.

Before anything had a soul,
While life was a heave of Matter, half inanimate,
This little bit chipped off in brilliance
And went whizzing through the slow, vast, succulent
    stems.

I believe there were no flowers then,
In the world where the humming-bird flashed ahead of
    creation.
I believe he pierced the slow vegetable veins with his long
    beak.
Probably he was big
As mosses, and little lizards, they say, were once big.
Probably he was a jabbing, terrifying monster.

We look at him through the wrong end of the long
    telescope of Time.

Luckily for us.

D. H. Lawrence

Minnows

*S*warms of minnows show their little heads,
Staying their wavy bodies 'gainst the streams,
To taste the luxury of sunny beams
Tempered with coolness. How they ever wrestle
With their own sweet delight, and ever nestle
Their silver bellies on the pebbly sand.
If you but scantily hold out the hand,
That very instant not one will remain;
But turn your eye, and they are there again.

from 'I stood tiptoe upon a little hill', John Keats

To a Fish of the Brook

*W*hy flyest thou away with fear?
Trust me there's naught of danger near,
    I have no wicked hook,
All covered with a snaring bait,
Alas, to tempt thee to thy fate,
    And drag thee from the brook.

Enjoy thy stream, O harmless fish;
And when an angler for his dish,
    Through gluttony's vile sin,
Attempts, a wretch, to pull thee *out*,
God give thee strength, O gentle trout,
    To pull the rascal *in*!

                    John Walcot

THE WHALE

Warm and buoyant in his oily mail
Gambols on seas of ice the unwieldy whale,
Wide waving fins round floating islands urge
His bulk gigantic through the troubled surge.

O'er the white wave he lifts his nostril bare,
And spouts transparent columns into the air;
The silvery arches catch the setting beams,
And transient rainbows tremble o'er the streams.

                                    Erasmus Darwin

LEVIATHAN

'Canst thou draw out leviathan with an hook?
Or his tongue with a cord which thou lettest down?
Canst thou put an hook into his nose?
Or bore his jaw through with a thorn? . . .
Who can open the doors of his face?
His teeth are terrible round about.
His scales are his pride,
Shut up together as with a close seal . . .
Out of his mouth go burning lamps,
And sparks of fire leap out.
Out of his nostrils goeth smoke,
As out of a seething pot or cauldron.
His breath kindleth coals,
And a flame goeth out of his mouth . . .
He maketh the deep to boil like a pot:
He maketh the sea like a pot of ointment.
He maketh a path to shine after him;
One would think the deep to be hoary.
Upon earth there is not his like,
Who is made without fear.
He beholdeth all high things:
He is a king over all the children of pride.'

from The Bible, The Book of Job

THE KRAKEN

Below the thunders of the upper deep;
Far far beneath in the abysmal sea,
His ancient, dreamless, uninvaded sleep
The Kraken sleepeth: faintest sunlights flee
About his shadowy sides: above him swell
Huge sponges of millennial growth and height;
And far away into the sickly light,
From many a wondrous grot and secret cell
Unnumber'd and enormous polypi
Winnow with giant fins the slumbering green.
There hath he lain for ages and will lie
Battening upon huge seaworms in his sleep,
Until the latter fire shall heat the deep;
Then once by men and angels to be seen,
In roaring he shall rise and on the surface die.

Alfred, Lord Tennyson

Upon the Snail

She goes but softly, but she goeth sure;
She stumbles not as stronger creatures do:
Her journey's shorter, so she may endure
Better than they which do much further go.

She makes no noise, but stilly seizeth on
The flower or herb appointed for her food,
The which she quietly doth feed upon,
While others range and gare, but find no good.

And though she doth but very softly go,
However 'tis not fast, nor slow, but sure;
And certainly they that do travel so,
The prize they do aim at, they do procure.

John Bunyan

CONSIDERING THE SNAIL

*T*he snail pushes through a green
night, for the grass is heavy
with water and meets over
the bright path he makes, where rain
has darkened the earth's dark. He
moves in a wood of desire,

pale antlers barely stirring
as he hunts. I cannot tell
what power is at work, drenched there
with purpose, knowing nothing.
What is a snail's fury? All
I think is that if later

I parted the blades above
the tunnel and saw the thin
trail of broken white across
litter, I would never have
imagined the slow passion
to that deliberate progress.

                              Thom Gunn

A Narrow Fellow in the Grass

A narrow fellow in the grass
Occasionally rides;
You may have met him – did you not?
His notice sudden is.

The grass divides as with a comb,
A spotted shaft is seen,
And then it closes at your feet
And opens further on.

He likes a boggy acre,
A floor too cool for corn;
Yet when a child and barefoot,
I more than once at noon

Have passed, I thought, a whiplash
Upbraiding in the sun;
When, stooping to secure it,
It wrinkled and was gone.

Several of nature's people
I know, and they know me;
I feel for them a transport
Of cordiality,

But never met this fellow,
Attended or alone,
Without a tighter breathing
And zero at the bone.

Emily Dickinson

THE VIPER

Barefoot I went and made no sound;
The earth was hot beneath:
The air was quivering around;
The circling kestrel eyed the ground
And hung above the heath.

There in the pathway stretched along
The lovely serpent lay:
She reared not up the heath among,
She bowed her head, she sheathed her tongue,
And shining stole away.

Fair was the brave embroidered dress,
Fairer the gold eyes shone:
Loving her not, yet did I bless
The fallen angel's comeliness;
And gazed when she had gone.

                                        Ruth Pitter

Snake

A snake came to my water-trough
On a hot, hot day, and I in pyjamas for the heat,
To drink there.

In the deep, strange-scented shade of the great dark carob-
    tree
I came down the steps with my pitcher
And must wait, must stand and wait, for there he was at
    the trough before me.

He reached down from a fissure in the earth-wall in the
    gloom
And trailed his yellow-brown slackness soft-bellied down,
    over the edge of the stone trough
And rested his throat upon the stone bottom,
And where the water had dripped from the tap, in a small
    clearness,
He sipped with his straight mouth,
Softly drank through his straight gums, into his slack long
    body,
Silently.

Someone was before me at my water-trough,
And I, like a second comer, waiting.

He lifted his head from his drinking, as cattle do,
And looked at me vaguely, as drinking cattle do,
And flickered his two-forked tongue from his lips, and
    mused a moment,

And stooped and drank a little more,
Being earth-brown, earth-golden from the burning bowels
    of the earth
On the day of Sicilian July, with Etna smoking.

The voice of my education said to me
He must be killed
For in Sicily the black, black snakes are innocent, the gold
    are venomous.
And voices in me said, If you were a man
You would take a stick and break him now, and finish
    him off.
But must I confess how I liked him,
How glad I was that he had come like a guest in quiet, to
    drink at my water-trough
And depart peaceful, pacified, and thankless,
Into the burning bowels of this earth?

Was it cowardice, that I dared not kill him?
Was it perversity, that I longed to talk to him?
Was it humility, to feel so honoured?
I felt so honoured.

And yet those voices:
If you were not afraid, you would kill him!

And truly I was afraid, I was most afraid,
But even so, honoured still more
That he should seek my hospitality
From out the dark door of the secret earth.

He drank enough
And lifted his head, dreamily, as one who has drunken,
And flickered his tongue like a forked night on the air, so
    black;
Seeming to lick his lips,
And looked around like a god, unseeing, into the air,
And slowly turned his head,
And slowly, very slowly, as if thrice adream,
Proceeded to draw his slow length curving round
And climb again the broken bank of my wall-face.
And as he put his head into that dreadful hole,
And as he slowly drew up, snake-easing his shoulders, and
    entered farther,
A sort of horror, a sort of protest against his withdrawing
    into that horrid black hole,
Deliberately going into the blackness, and slowly drawing
    himself after,
Overcame me now his back was turned.

I looked round, I put down my pitcher,
I picked up a clumsy log
And threw it at the water-trough with a clatter.

I think it did not hit him,
But suddenly that part of him that was left behind
    convulsed in undignified haste,
Writhed like lightning, and was gone
Into the black hole, the earth-lipped fissure in the wall-
    front,
At which, in the intense still noon, I stared with
    fascination.

And immediately I regretted it.
I thought how paltry, how vulgar, what a mean act!
I despised myself and the voices of my accursed human
    education.

And I thought of the albatross,
And I wished he would come back, my snake.
For he seemed to me again like a king,
Like a king in exile, uncrowned in the underworld,
Now due to be crowned again.

And so, I missed my chance with one of the lords
Of life.
And I have something to expiate;
A pettiness.

                                        D. H. Lawrence

The Ants

What wonder strikes the curious, while he views
   The black ant's city, by a rotten tree,
Or woodland bank! In ignorance we muse:
   Pausing, annoyed, – we know not what we see,
Such government and thought there seem to be;
Some looking on, and urging some to toil,
   Dragging their loads of bent-stalks slavishly:
And what's more wonderful, when big loads foil
   One ant or two to carry, quickly then
A swarm flock round to help their fellow-men.
   Surely they speak a language whisperingly,
Too fine for us to hear, and sure their ways
   Prove they have kings and laws, and that they be
Deformèd remnants of the Fairy-days.

John Clare

The Fly

Little Fly,
Thy summer's play
My thoughtless hand
Has brushed away.

Am not I
A fly like thee?
Or art not thou
A man like me?

For I dance,
And drink, and sing,
Till some blind hand
Shall brush my wing.

If thought is life
And strength and breath,
And the want
Of thought is death;

Then am I
A happy fly,
If I live
Or if I die.

William Blake

Today I Saw the Dragon-fly

*T*oday I saw the dragon-fly
Come from the wells where he did lie.

An inner impulse rent the veil
Of his old husk: from head to tail
Came out clear plates of sapphire mail.
He dried his wings: like gauze they grew;
Through crofts and pastures wet with dew
A living flash of light he flew.

Alfred, Lord Tennyson

Grasshoppers

*G*rasshoppers go in many a thrumming spring
And now to stalks of tasselled sour-grass cling,
That shakes and sways a while, but still keeps straight;
While arching oxeye doubles with his weight.
Next on the cat-tail grass with farther bound
He springs, that bends until they touch the ground.

John Clare

An August Midnight

A shaded lamp and a waving blind,
And the beat of a clock from a distant floor:
On this scene enter – winged, horned, and spined –
A longlegs, a moth, and a dumbledore;
While 'mid my page there idly stands
A sleepy fly, that rubs its hands . . .

Thus meet we five, in this still place,
At this point of time, at this point in space.
– My guests besmear my new-penned line,
Or bang at the lamp and fall supine.
'God's humblest, they!' I muse. Yet why?
They know Earth-secrets that know not I.

Thomas Hardy

Very Remarkable
Beasts

MACAVITY: THE MYSTERY CAT

Macavity's a Mystery Cat: he's called the Hidden Paw —
For he's the master criminal who can defy the Law.
He's the bafflement of Scotland Yard, the Flying Squad's
    despair:
For when they reach the scene of crime — *Macavity's not
    there!*

Macavity, Macavity, there's no-one like Macavity,
He's broken every human law, he breaks the law of
    gravity.
His powers of levitation would make a fakir stare,
And when you reach the scene of crime — *Macavity's not
    there!*
You may seek him in the basement, you may look up in
    the air —
But I tell you once and once again, *Macavity's not there!*

Macavity's a ginger cat, he's very tall and thin;
You would know him if you saw him, for his eyes are
    sunken in.
His brow is deeply lined with thought, his head is highly
    domed;
His coat is dusty from neglect, his whiskers are uncombed.
He sways his head from side to side, with movements like
    a snake;
And when you think he's half asleep, he's always wide
    awake.

Macavity, Macavity, there's no one like Macavity,
For he's a fiend in feline shape, a monster of depravity.
You may meet him in a by-street, you may see him in the
    square –
But when a crime's discovered, then *Macavity's not there!*

He's outwardly respectable. (They say he cheats at cards.)
And his footprints are not found in any file of Scotland
    Yard's.
And when the larder's looted, or the jewel-case is rifled,
Or when the milk is missing, or another peke's been
    stifled,
Or the greenhouse glass is broken, and the trellis past
    repair –
Ay, there's the wonder of the thing! *Macavity's not there!*
And when the Foreign Office find a Treaty's gone astray,
Or the Admiralty lose some plans and drawings by the
    way,
There may be a scrap of paper in the hall or on the stair –
But it's useless to investigate – *Macavity's not there!*
And when the loss has been disclosed, the Secret Service
    say:
'It *must* have been Macavity!' – but he's a mile away.
You'll be sure to find him resting, or a-licking of his
    thumbs,
Or engaged in doing complicated long division sums.

Macavity, Macavity, there's no-one like Macavity,
There never was a Cat of such deceitfulness and suavity.
He always has an alibi, and one or two to spare:
At whatever time the deed took place – MACAVITY
   WASN'T THERE!
And they say that all the Cats whose wicked deeds are
   widely known
(I might mention Mungojerrie, I might mention
   Griddlebone)
Are nothing more than agents for the Cat who all the time
Just controls their operations: the Napoleon of Crime!

                                                   T. S. Eliot

THE OWL AND THE PUSSY-CAT

The Owl and the Pussy-Cat went to sea
    In a beautiful pea-green boat,
They took some honey, and plenty of money,
    Wrapped up in a five-pound note.
The Owl looked up to the stars above,
    And sang to a small guitar,
'O lovely Pussy! O Pussy, my love,
    What a beautiful Pussy you are,
        You are,
        You are!
    What a beautiful Pussy you are!'

Pussy said to the Owl, 'You elegant fowl!
    How charmingly sweet you sing!
O let us be married! too long we have tarried
    But what shall we do for a ring?'
They sailed away for a year and a day,
    To the land where the Bong-tree grows,
And there in a wood a Piggy-wig stood,
    With a ring at the end of his nose,
        His nose,
        His nose,
    With a ring at the end of his nose.

'Dear Pig, are you willing to sell for one shilling
  Your ring?' Said the Piggy, 'I will.'
So they took it away, and were married next day
  By the Turkey who lives on the hill.
They dined on mince, and slices of quince,
  Which they ate with a runcible spoon;
And hand in hand, on the edge of the sand,
  They danced by the light of the moon,
    The moon,
    The moon,
  They danced by the light of the moon.

Edward Lear

THE TERMITE

Some primal termite knocked on wood
And tasted it and found it good,
And that is why your cousin May
Fell through the parlour floor today.

Ogden Nash

JABBERWOCKY

'Twas brillig, and the slithy toves
　　Did gyre and gimble in the wabe;
All mimsy were the borogroves,
　　And the mome raths outgrabe.

'Beware the Jabberwock, my son!
　　The jaws that bite, the claws that catch!
Beware the Jubjub bird, and shun
　　The frumious Bandersnatch!'

He took his vorpal sword in hand:
　　Long time the manxome foe he sought –
So rested he by the Tumtum tree,
　　And stood awhile in thought.

And, as in uffish thought he stood,
　　The Jabberwock, with eyes of flame,
Came whiffling through the tulgy wood,
　　And burbled as it came!

One, two! One, two! And through and through
　　The vorpal blade went snicker-snack!
He left it dead, and with its head
　　He went galumphing back.

'And hast thou slain the Jabberwock?
   Come to my arms, my beamish boy!
O frabjous day! Callooh! Callay!'
   He chortled in his joy.

'Twas brillig, and the slithy toves
   Did gyre and gimble in the wabe:
All mimsy were the borogroves,
   And the mome raths outgrabe.

                Lewis Carroll

A QUESTION OF SCALE

So, naturalists observe, a flea
Hath smaller fleas that on him prey;
And these have smaller fleas to bite 'em,
And so proceed *ad infinitum*.

                Jonathan Swift

THE SNITTERJIPE

In mellowy orchards, rich and ripe,
Is found the luminous Snitterjipe.
Bad boys who climb the bulging trees
Feel his sharp breath about their knees;
His trembling whiskers tickle so,
They squeak and squeal till they let go.
They hear his far-from-friendly bark;
They see his eyeballs in the dark
Shining and shifting in their sockets
As round and big as pears in pockets.
They feel his hot and wrinkly hide;
They see his nostrils flaming wide,
His tapering teeth, his jutting jaws,
His tongue, his tail, his twenty claws.
His hairy shadow in the moon
It makes them sweat, it makes them swoon;
And as they climb the orchard wall,
They let their pilfered pippins fall.
The Snitterjipe suspends pursuit
And falls upon the fallen fruit;
And while they flee the monster fierce,
Apples, not boys, his talons pierce.
With thumping hearts they hear him munch –
Six apples at a time he'll crunch.
At length he falls asleep, and they
On tiptoe take their homeward way.
But long before the blackbirds pipe
To welcome day, the Snitterjipe
Has fled afar, and on the green
Only his fearsome prints are seen.

James Reeves

A Small Dragon

I've found a small dragon in the woodshed.
Think it must have come from deep inside a forest
because it's damp and green and leaves
are still reflecting in its eyes.

I fed it on many things, tried grass,
the roots of stars, hazelnut and dandelion,
but it stared up at me as if to say, I need
food you can't provide.

It made a nest among the coal,
not unlike a bird's but larger,
it's out of place here
and is quite silent.

If you believed in it I would come
hurrying to your house to let you share my wonder,
but I want instead to see
if you yourself will pass this way.

                                  Brian Patten

GHOSTS, GHOULS AND WITCHES

THE WITCHES ARE HERE

Look out! Look out, boys! Clear the track!
The witches are here! They've all come back!
They hanged them high – No use! No use!
What cares a witch for the hangman's noose?
They buried them deep, but they wouldn't lie still,
For cats and witches are hard to kill;
They swore they shouldn't and wouldn't die –
Books said they did, but they lie! they lie!

Oliver Wendell Holmes

from WITCHES' SONG

The owl is abroad, the bat and the toad,
   And so is the cat-a-mountain;
The ant and the mole sit both in a hole,
   And frog peeps out o' the fountain;
The dogs they do bay, and the timbrels play,
   The spindle is now a-turning;
The moon it is red, and the stars are fled,
   And all the sky is a-burning.

Ben Jonson

THE WANDERING SPECTRE

Wae's me, wae's me,
The acorn's not yet
Fallen from the tree
That's to grow the wood,
That's to make the cradle,
That's to rock the bairn,
That's to grow a man,
That's to lay me.

Anonymous

The Ghosts' High Noon

When the night wind howls in the chimney cowls, and
   the bat in the moonlight flies,
And inky clouds, like funeral shrouds, sail over the
   midnight skies –
When the footpads quail at the night-bird's wail, and black
   dogs bay the moon,
Then is the spectres' holiday – then is the ghosts' high noon!

As the sob of the breeze sweeps over the trees, and the
   mists lie low on the fen,
From grey tombstones are gathered the bones that once
   were women and men,
And away they go, with a mop and a mow, to the revel
   that ends too soon,
For cockcrow limits our holiday – the dead of the night's
   high noon!

And then each ghost with his ladye-toast to their
   churchyard beds take flight,
With a kiss, perhaps, on her lantern chaps, and a grisly
   grim 'good night';
Till the welcome knell of the midnight bell rings forth its
   jolliest tune,
And ushers our next high holiday – the dead of the night's
   high noon!

W. S. Gilbert

WITCHES' CHANT

Round about the cauldron go:
In the poisoned entrails throw.
Toad, that under cold stone
Days and nights has thirty-one
Sweated venom sleeping got,
Boil thou first in the charmèd pot.
   Double, double toil and trouble;
   Fire burn and cauldron bubble.

Fillet of a fenny snake,
In the cauldron boil and bake;
Eye of newt and toe of frog,
Wool of bat and tongue of dog,
Adder's fork and blindworm's sting,
Lizard's leg and owlet's wing.
For a charm of powerful trouble,
Like a hell-broth boil and bubble.
   Double, double toil and trouble;
   Fire burn and cauldron bubble.

Scale of dragon, tooth of wolf,
Witch's mummy, maw and gulf
Of the ravenous salt-sea shark,
Root of hemlock digged in the dark,
Make the gruel thick and slab:
Add thereto a tiger's chaudron,
For the ingredients of our cauldron.
   Double, double toil and trouble,
   Fire burn and cauldron bubble.

from Macbeth, William Shakespeare

THE GHOUL

*T*he gruesome ghoul, the grisly ghoul,
without the slightest noise
waits patiently beside the school
to feast on girls and boys.

He lunges fiercely through the air
as they come out to play,
then grabs a couple by the hair
and drags them far away.

He cracks their bones and snaps their backs
and squeezes out their lungs,
he chews their thumbs like candy snacks
and pulls apart their tongues.

He slices their stomachs and bites their heart
and tears their flesh to shreds,
he swallows their toes like toasted tarts
and gobbles down their heads.

Fingers, elbows, hands and knees
and arms and legs and feet –
he eats them with delight and ease,
for every part's a treat.

And when the gruesome, grisly ghoul
has nothing left to chew,
he hurries to another school
and waits . . . perhaps for you.

Jack Prelutsky

THE VISITOR

A crumbling churchyard, the sea and the moon;
The waves had gouged out grave and bone;
A man was walking, late and alone . . .

He saw a skeleton on the ground;
A ring on a bony finger he found.

He ran home to his wife and gave her the ring.
'Oh, where did you get it?' He said not a thing.

'It's the loveliest ring in the world,' she said,
As it glowed on her finger. They slipped off to bed.

At midnight they woke. In the dark outside,
'Give me my ring!' a chill voice cried.

'What was that, William? What did it say?'
'Don't worry, my dear. It'll soon go away.'

'I'm coming!' A skeleton opened the door.
'Give me my ring!' It was crossing the floor.

'What was that, William? What did it say?'
'Don't worry, my dear. It'll soon go away.'

'I'm reaching you now! I'm climbing the bed.'
The wife pulled the sheet right over her head.

It was torn from her grasp and tossed in the air:
'I'll drag you out of bed by the hair!'

'What was that, William? What did it say?'
'Throw the ring through the window! THROW IT
    AWAY!'

She threw it. The skeleton leapt from the sill,
And into the night it clattered downhill,
Fainter . . . and fainter . . . Then all was still.

Ian Serraillier

A Cornish Charm

*F*rom Ghosties and Ghoulies
And long-leggity Beasties,
And all things that go BUMP
in the night –
Good Lord, deliver us!

Anonymous

Charm

*B*ring the holy crust of bread,
Lay it underneath the head;
'Tis a certain charm to keep
Hags away, while children sleep.

Robert Herrick

The Sea

SEA FEVER

I must go down to the seas again, to the lonely sea and
    the sky,
And all I ask is a tall ship and a star to steer her by,
And the wheel's kick and the wind's song and the white
    sail's shaking,
And a grey mist on the sea's face, and a grey dawn
    breaking.

I must go down to the seas again, for the call of the
    running tide
Is a wild call and a clear call that may not be denied;
And all I ask is a windy day with the white clouds flying,
And the flung spray and the blown spume, and the sea-
    gulls crying.

I must go down to the seas again, to the vagrant gypsy
    life,
To the gull's way and the whale's way where the wind's
    like a whetted knife;
And all I ask is a merry yarn from a laughing fellow-rover,
And quiet sleep and a sweet dream when the long trick's
    over.

                            John Masefield

from DOVER BEACH

The sea is calm to-night.
The tide is full, the moon lies fair
Upon the straits; – on the French coast the light
Gleams and is gone; the cliffs of England stand,
Glimmering and vast, out in the tranquil bay.
Come to the window, sweet is the night air.
Only, from the long line of spray
Where the sea meets the moon-blanched land,
Listen! you hear the grating roar
Of pebbles which the waves draw back, and fling,
At their return, up the high strand,
Begin, and cease, and then again begin,
With tremulous cadence slow, and bring
The eternal note of sadness in . . .

Matthew Arnold

SPRAY

It is a wonder foam is so beautiful.
A wave bursts in anger on a rock, broken up
in wild white sibilant spray
and falls back, drawing in its breath with rage,
with frustration how beautiful!

D. H. Lawrence

from THE SEAFARER

*P*rosperous men,
Living on land, do not begin to understand
How I, careworn and cut off from my kinsmen,
Have as an exile endured the winter
On the icy sea . . .
Icicles hung round me; hail showers flew.
The only sound here, was of the sea booming –
The ice-cold wave – and at times the song of the swan.
The cry of the gannet was all my gladness,
The call of the curlew, not the laughter of men,
The mewing gull, not the sweetness of mead.
There, storms echoed off the rocky cliffs; the icy-feathered
    tern
Answered them; and often the eagle,
Dewy-winged, screeched overhead.

Anonymous, translated from the Anglo-Saxon
by Kevin Crossley-Holland

THE WORKS OF THE LORD

They that go down to the sea in ships,
That do business in great waters,
These see the works of the LORD
And his wonders in the deep.
For he commandeth, and raiseth the stormy wind,
Which lifteth up the waves thereof.
They mount up to the heaven, they go down again to the
    depth;
Their soul melteth away because of trouble.
They reel to and fro, and stagger like a drunken man,
And are at their wits' end.
Then they cry unto the LORD in their trouble,
And he bringeth them out of their distresses.
He maketh the storm a calm,
So that the waves thereof are still.

from The Bible, Psalm 107

THE GALLANT SHIP

Upon the gale she stooped her side,
And bounded o'er the swelling tide,
    As she were dancing home;
The merry seamen laughed to see
Their gallant ship so lustily
    Furrow the sea-green foam.

Sir Walter Scott

A Wet Sheet and a Flowing Sea

A wet sheet and a flowing sea,
A wind that follows fast,
And fills the white and rustling sail,
   And bends the gallant mast –
And bends the gallant mast, my boys,
   While, like the eagle free,
Away the good ship flies, and leaves
   Old England on the lee.

O for a soft and gentle wind!
   I heard a fair one cry;
But give to me the snoring breeze
   And white waves heaving high –
And white waves heaving high, my boys,
   The good ship tight and free;
The world of waters is our home,
   And merry men are we.

There's tempest in yon hornèd moon
   And lightning in yon cloud;
And hark the music, mariners!
   The wind is piping loud –
The wind is piping loud, my boys,
   The lightning flashes free,
While the hollow oak our palace is,
   Our heritage the sea.

Allan Cunningham

from THE RIME OF THE ANCIENT MARINER

The fair breeze blew, the white foam flew,
The furrow streamed off free:
We were the first that ever burst
Into that silent sea.

Down dropt the breeze, the sails dropt down,
'Twas sad as sad could be;
And we did speak only to break
The silence of the sea!

All in a hot and copper sky,
The bloody Sun, at noon,
Right up above the mast did stand,
No bigger than the Moon.

Day after day, day after day,
We stuck, nor breath nor motion;
As idle as a painted ship
Upon a painted ocean.

Water, water, every where,
And all the boards did shrink;
Water, water, every where,
Nor any drop to drink.

The very deep did rot: O Christ!
That ever this should be!
Yea, slimy things did crawl with legs
Upon the slimy sea.

About, about, in reel and rout
The death-fires danced at night;
The water, like a witch's oils,
Burnt green, and blue and white.

Samuel Taylor Coleridge

THE MOON IS UP

The moon is up: the stars are bright:
    The wind is fresh and free!
We're out to seek for gold tonight
    Across the silver sea!
The world is growing grey and old:
    Break out the sails again!
We're out to seek a Realm of Gold
    Beyond the Spanish Main.

We're sick of all the cringing knees,
    The courtly smiles and lies!
God, let thy singing Channel breeze
    Lighten our hearts and eyes!
Let love no more be bought and sold
    For earthly loss or gain;
We're out to seek an Age of Gold
    Beyond the Spanish Main.

Beyond the light of far Cathay,
    Beyond all mortal dreams,
Beyond the reach of night and day
    Our El Dorado gleams,
Revealing – as the skies unfold –
    A star without a stain,
The Glory of the Gates of Gold
    Beyond the Spanish Main.

Alfred Noyes

THE PRESS-GANG

Here's the tender coming,
  Pressing all the men;
    O, dear honey,
  What shall we do then?
Here's the tender coming,
  Off at Shields Bar.
Here's the tender coming,
  Full of men of war.

Here's the tender coming,
  Stealing of my dear;
    O, dear honey,
They'll ship you out of here,
  They'll ship you foreign,
For that is what it means.
Here's the tender coming,
Full of red marines.

                    Anonymous

A BURNT SHIP

Out of a fired ship, which, by no way
But drowning, could be rescued from the flame,
Some men leaped forth, and ever as they came
Near the foe's ships, did by their shot decay;
So all were lost, which in the ship were found,
They in the sea being burnt, they in the burnt ship
  drowned.

John Donne

What Pain It Was to Drown

O lord, methought what pain it was to drown,
What dreadful noise of waters in mine ears,
What sights of ugly death within mine eyes!
Methought I saw a thousand fearful wrecks:
A thousand men that fishes gnawed upon,
Wedges of gold, great anchors, heaps of pearl,
Inestimable stones, unvalued jewels,
All scattered in the bottom of the sea:
Some lay in dead men's skulls, and in the holes
Where eyes did once inhabit, there were crept,
As 'twere in scorn of eyes, reflecting gems,
That wooed the slimy bottom of the deep,
    And mocked the dead bones that lay scattered by.

from Richard III, William Shakespeare

THE SHIP

There was no song nor shout of joy
   Nor beam of moon or sun,
When she came back from the voyage
   Long ago begun;
But twilight on the waters
   Was quiet and grey,
And she glided steady, steady and pensive,
   Over the open bay.

Her sails were brown and ragged,
   And her crew hollow-eyed,
But their silent lips spoke content
   And their shoulders pride;
Though she had no captives on her deck,
   And in her hold
There were no heaps of corn or timber
   Or silks or gold.

J. C. Squire

The Dismantled Ship

In some unused lagoon, some nameless bay,
On sluggish, lonesome waters, anchored near the shore,
An old, dismasted, grey and battered ship, disabled, done,
After free voyages to all the seas of earth, hauled up at last
   and hawsered tight,
Lies rusting, mouldering.

Walt Whitman

THE SANDS OF DEE

'O Mary, go and call the cattle home,
    And call the cattle home,
    And call the cattle home
  Across the sands of Dee;'
The western wind was wild and dank with foam,
  And all alone went she.

The western tide crept up along the sand,
    And o'er and o'er the sand,
    And round and round the sand,
  As far as eye could see.
The rolling mist came down and hid the land:
  And never home came she.

'Oh, is it weed, or fish, or floating hair
    A tress of golden hair,
    A drownèd maiden's hair
  Above the nets at sea?
Was never salmon yet that shone so fair
  Among the stakes on Dee.'

They rowed her in across the rolling foam,
    The cruel, crawling foam,
    The cruel, hungry foam,
  To her grave beside the sea:
But still the boatmen hear her call the cattle home,
  Across the sands of Dee.

Charles Kingsley

Full Fathom Five

Full fathom five thy father lies;
  Of his bones are coral made;
Those are pearls that were his eyes:
  Nothing of him that doth fade,
But doth suffer a sea-change
Into something rich and strange.
Sea-nymphs hourly ring his knell:
      Ding-dong.
  Hark! now I hear them –
      Ding-dong, bell!

from The Tempest, William Shakespeare

BREAK, BREAK, BREAK

Break, break, break,
  On thy cold grey stones, O Sea!
And I would that my tongue could utter
  The thoughts that arise in me.

O well for the fisherman's boy,
  That he shouts with his sister at play!
O well for the sailor lad,
  That he sings in his boat on the bay!

And the stately ships go on
  To their haven under the hill;
But O for the touch of a vanish'd hand,
  And the sound of a voice that is still!

Break, break, break,
  At the foot of thy crags, O Sea!
But the tender grace of a day that is dead
  Will never come back to me.

Alfred, Lord Tennyson

MYSTERY, DREAMS AND ENCHANTMENTS

The Way Through the Woods

*T*hey shut the way through the woods
Seventy years ago.
Weather and rain have undone it again,
And now you would never know
There was once a road through the woods
Before they planted the trees.
It is underneath the coppice and heath,
And the thin anemones.
Only the keeper sees
That, where the ring-dove broods,
And the badgers roll at ease,
There was once a road through the woods.

Yet, if you enter the woods
Of a summer evening late,
When the night-air cools on the trout-ringed pools
Where the otter whistles his mate,
(They fear not men in the woods,
Because they see so few)
You will hear the beat of a horse's feet,
And the swish of a skirt in the dew,
Steadily cantering through
The misty solitudes,
As though they perfectly knew
The old lost road through the woods . . .
But there is no road through the woods.

Rudyard Kipling

THE EXPLOSION

On the day of the explosion
Shadows pointed towards the pithead:
In the sun the slagheap slept.

Down the lane came men in pitboots
Coughing oath-edged talk and pipe-smoke,
Shouldering off the freshened silence.

One chased after rabbits; lost them;
Came back with a nest of lark's eggs;
Showed them; lodged them in the grasses.

So they passed in beards and moleskins,
Fathers, brothers, nicknames, laughter,
Through the tall gates standing open.

At noon, there came a tremor; cows
Stopped chewing for a second; sun,
Scarfed as in a heat-haze, dimmed.

The dead go on before us, they
Are sitting in God's house in comfort,
We shall see them face to face —

Plain as lettering in the chapels
It was said, and for a second
Wives saw men of the explosion

Larger than in life they managed –
Gold as on a coin, or walking
Somehow from the sun towards them,

One showing the eggs unbroken.

Philip Larkin

ECHO

'*W*ho called?' I said, and the words
Through the whispering glades,
Hither, thither, baffled the birds –
   'Who called? Who called?'

The leafy boughs on high
   Hissed in the sun;
The dark air carried my cry
   Faintingly on:

Eyes in the green, in the shade,
   In the motionless brake,
Voices that said what I said,
   For mockery's sake:

'Who cares?' I bawled through my tears:
   The wind fell low:
In the silence, 'Who cares? who cares?'
   Wailed to and fro.

Walter de la Mare

THE LISTENERS

'Is there anybody there?' said the Traveller,
Knocking on the moonlit door;
And his horse in the silence champed the grasses
Of the forest's ferny floor:
And a bird flew up out of the turret,
Above the Traveller's head:
And he smote upon the door again a second time;
'Is there anybody there?' he said.
But no one descended to the Traveller;
No head from the leaf-fringed sill
Leaned over and looked into his grey eyes,
Where he stood perplexed and still.
But only a host of phantom listeners
That dwelt in the lone house then
Stood listening in the quiet of the moonlight
To that voice from the world of men:
Stood thronging the faint moonbeams on the dark stair,
That goes down to the empty hall,
Hearkening in an air stirred and shaken
By the lonely Traveller's call.
And he felt in his heart their strangeness,
Their stillness answering his cry,
While his horse moved, cropping the dark turf,
'Neath the starred and leafy sky;
For he suddenly smote on the door, even
Louder, and lifted his head:
'Tell them I came, and no one answered,
That I kept my word,' he said.
Never the least stir made the listeners,
Though every word he spake

Fell echoing through the shadowiness of the still house
From the one man left awake:
Ay, they heard his foot upon the stirrup,
And the sound of iron on stone,
And how the silence surged softly backward,
When the plunging hoofs were gone.

                              Walter de la Mare

Middle Ages

I heard a clash, and a cry,
And a horseman fleeing the wood.
The moon hid in a cloud.
Deep in shadow I stood.
　'Ugly work!' thought I,
Holding my breath.
　'*Men must be cruel and proud,*
Jousting for death.'

With gusty glimmering shone
The moon; and the wind blew colder.
A man went over the hill,
Bent to his horse's shoulder.
　'*Time for me to be gone.*' . . .
Darkly I fled.
Owls in the wood were shrill,
And the moon sank red.

Siegfried Sassoon

Ghosts

I to a crumpled cabin came
Upon a hillside high,
And with me was a withered dame
As weariful as I.
'It used to be our home,' said she;
'How I remember well!
Oh that our happy hearth should be
Today an empty shell!'

The door was flailing in the storm
That deafed us with its din;
The roof that kept us once so warm
Now let the snow-drift in.
The floor sagged to the sod below,
The walls caved crazily;
We only heard the wind of woe
Where once was glow and glee.

So there we stood disconsolate
Beneath the Midnight Dome,
An ancient miner and his mate,
Before our wedded home,
Where we had known such love and cheer . . .
I sighed, then soft she said:
'Do not regret – remember, dear,
We, too, are dead.'

Robert Service

A Spell for Creation

Within the flower there lies a seed,
Within the seed there springs a tree,
Within the tree there spreads a wood.

In the wood there burns a fire,
And in the fire there melts a stone,
Within the stone a ring of iron.

Within the ring there lies an O,
Within the O there looks an eye,
In the eye there swims a sea,

And in the sea reflected sky,
And in the sky there shines the sun,
Within the sun a bird of gold.

Within the bird there beats a heart,
And from the heart there flows a song,
And in the song there sings a word.

In the word there speaks a world,
A world of joy, a world of grief,
From joy and grief there springs my love.

Oh love, my love, there springs a world,
And on the world there shines a sun,
And in the sun there burns a fire,

Within the fire consumes my heart,
And in my heart there beats a bird,
And in the bird there wakes an eye,
Within the eye, earth, sea and sky,
Earth, sky and sea within an O
Lie like the seed within the flower.

Kathleen Raine

I GIVE YOU THE END OF A GOLDEN STRING

I give you the end of a golden string;
   Only wind it into a ball,
It will lead you in at Heaven's gate,
   Built in Jerusalem's wall.

William Blake

KUBLA KHAN

*I*n Xanadu did Kubla Khan
A stately pleasure-dome decree:
Where Alph, the sacred river, ran
Through caverns measureless to man
　Down to a sunless sea.
So twice five miles of fertile ground
With walls and towers were girdled round:
And there were gardens bright with sinuous rills,
Where blossomed many an incense-bearing tree;
And here were forests ancient as the hills,
Enfolding sunny spots of greenery.

But oh! that deep romantic chasm which slanted
Down the green hill athwart a cedarn cover!
A savage place! as holy and enchanted
As e'er beneath a waning moon was haunted
By woman wailing for her demon-lover!
And from this chasm, with ceaseless turmoil seething,
As if this earth in fast thick pants were breathing,
A mighty fountain momently was forced:
Amid whose swift half-intermitted burst
Huge fragments vaulted like rebounding hail,
Or chaffy grain beneath the thresher's flail:
And 'mid these dancing rocks at once and ever
It flung up momently the sacred river.
Five miles meandering with a mazy motion
Through wood and dale the sacred river ran,
Then reached the caverns measureless to man,
And sank in tumult to a lifeless ocean:

And 'mid this tumult Kubla heard from far
Ancestral voices prophesying war!
   The shadow of the dome of pleasure
   Floated midway on the waves;
   Where was heard the mingled measure
   From the fountain and the caves.
It was a miracle of rare device,
A sunny pleasure-dome with caves of ice!

   A damsel with a dulcimer
   In a vision once I saw:
   It was an Abyssinian maid,
   And on her dulcimer she played,
   Singing of Mount Abora.
   Could I revive within me
   Her symphony and song,
To such a deep delight 'twould win me
That with music loud and long,
I would build that dome in air,
That sunny dome! those caves of ice!
And all who heard should see them there,
And all should cry, Beware! Beware!
His flashing eyes, his floating hair!
Weave a circle round him thrice,
And close your eyes with holy dread,
For he on honey-dew hath fed,
And drunk the milk of Paradise.

          Samuel Taylor Coleridge

THE SPLENDOUR FALLS

*T*he splendour falls on castle walls
     And snowy summits old in story:
The long light shakes across the lakes,
     And the wild cataract leaps in glory.
Blow, bugle, blow, set the wild echoes flying,
Blow, bugle; answer, echoes, dying, dying, dying.

O hark, O hear! how thin and clear,
     And thinner, clearer, farther going!
O sweet and far from cliff and scar
     The horns of Elfland faintly blowing!
Blow, let us hear the purple glens replying:
Blow, bugle; answer, echoes, dying, dying, dying.

O love, they die in yon rich sky,
     They faint on hill or field or river:
Our echoes roll from soul to soul,
     And grow for ever and for ever.
Blow, bugle, blow, set the wild echoes flying,
And answer, echoes, answer, dying, dying, dying.

                              Alfred, Lord Tennyson

The Song of Wandering Aengus

I went out to the hazel wood,
Because a fire was in my head,
And cut and peeled a hazel wand,
And hooked a berry to a thread;
And when white moths were on the wing,
And moth-like stars were flickering out,
I dropped the berry in a stream
And caught a little silver trout.

When I had laid it on the floor
I went to blow the fire a-flame,
But something rustled on the floor,
And someone called me by my name:
It had become a glimmering girl
With apple blossom in her hair
Who called me by my name and ran
And faded through the brightening air.

Though I am old with wandering
Through hollow lands and hilly lands,
I will find out where she has gone,
And kiss her lips and take her hands;
And walk among long dappled grass,
And pluck till time and times are done
The silver apples of the moon,
The golden apples of the sun.

William Butler Yeats

ETERNITY

I saw Eternity the other night
Like a great Ring of pure and endless light,
    All calm, as it was bright;
And round beneath it, Time in hours, days, years,
    Driven by the spheres
Like a vast shadow moved, in which the world
    And all her train were hurled.

Henry Vaughan

from AUGURIES OF INNOCENCE

To see a World in a Grain of Sand
And a Heaven in a Wild Flower,
Hold Infinity in the palm of your hand
And Eternity in an hour.

William Blake

ENCHANTED ISLAND

The isle is full of noises,
Sounds, and sweet airs, that give delight, and hurt not.
Sometimes a thousand twangling instruments
Will hum about mine ears; and sometimes voices,
That, if I then had wak'd after long sleep,
Will make me sleep again; and then, in dreaming,
The clouds methought would open and show riches
Ready to drop upon me; that, when I wak'd,
I cried to dream again.

from The Tempest, William Shakespeare

La Belle Dame sans Merci

O what can ail thee, Knight-at-arms,
  Alone and palely loitering?
The sedge is wither'd from the lake,
  And no birds sing.

O what can ail thee, Knight-at-arms,
  So haggard and so woe-begone?
The squirrel's granary is full,
  And the harvest's done.

I see a lily on thy brow
  With anguish moist and fever dew;
And on thy cheeks a fading rose
  Fast withereth too.

I met a Lady in the meads,
  Full beautiful, a faery's child; —
Her hair was long, her foot was light,
  And her eyes were wild.

I made a garland for her head,
  And bracelets too, and fragrant zone;
She look'd at me as she did love,
  And made sweet moan.

I set her on my pacing steed,
  And nothing else saw all day long;
For sidelong would she lean, and sing
  A faery's song.

She found me roots of relish sweet,
And honey wild, and manna dew;
And sure in language strange she said –
'I love thee true!'

She took me to her elfin grot,
And there she wept and sigh'd full sore,
And there I shut her wild, wild eyes
With kisses four.

And there she lullèd me asleep,
And then I dream'd – Ah! woe betide!
The latest dream I ever dream'd,
On the cold hill-side.

I saw pale kings and princes too,
Pale warriors, death-pale were they all;
They cried – 'La Belle Dame sans Merci
Hath thee in thrall!'
I saw their starv'd lips in the gloam,
With horrid warning gapèd wide,
And I awoke, and found me here
On the cold hill-side.

And this is why I sojourn here
Alone and palely loitering,
Though the sedge is withered from the lake,
And no birds sing.

John Keats

O Child Beside the Waterfall

O Child beside the Waterfall
what songs without a word
rise from those waters like the call
only a heart has heard –
the Joy, the Joy in all things
rise whistling like a bird.

O Child beside the Waterfall
I hear them too, the brief
heavenly notes, the harp of dawn,
the nightingale on the leaf,
all, all dispel the darkness and
the silence of our grief.

O Child beside the Waterfall
I see you standing there
with waterdrops and fireflies
and hummingbirds in the air,
all singing praise of paradise,
paradise everywhere.

George Barker

EGYPT'S MIGHT IS TUMBLED DOWN

Egypt's might is tumbled down
   Down a-down the deeps of thought;
Greece is fallen and Troy town,
Glorious Rome hath lost her crown,
     Venice' pride is nought.

But the dreams their children dreamed
   Fleeting, unsubstantial, vain,
Shadowy as the shadows seemed,
Airy nothing, as they deemed,
     These remain.

Mary Coleridge

LOVE'S MOODS

Meeting at Night

*T*he grey sea and the long black land;
And the yellow half-moon large and low;
And the startled little waves that leap
In fiery ringlets from their sleep,
As I gain the cove with pushing prow,
And quench its speed i' the slushy sand.

Then a mile of warm sea-scented beach;
Three fields to cross till a farm appears;
A tap at the pane, the quick sharp scratch
And blue spurt of a lighted match,
And a voice less loud, through its joys and fears,
Than the two hearts beating each to each!

Robert Browning

My True Love

My true love hath my heart, and I have his,
   By just exchange, one for the other given.
I hold his dear, and mine he cannot miss:
   There never was a better bargain driven.

His heart in me, keeps me and him in one,
   My heart in him, his thoughts and senses guides:
He loves my heart, for once it was his own:
   I cherish his, because in me it bides.

His heart his wound receivèd from my sight:
   My heart was wounded, with his wounded heart,
For as from me, on him his hurt did light,
   So still methought in me his hurt did smart:
     Both equal hurt, in this change sought our bliss:
     My true love hath my heart and I have his.

Sir Philip Sidney

To My Dear and Loving Husband

If ever two were one, then surely we.
If ever man were loved by wife, then thee;
If ever wife was happy in a man,
Compare with me, ye women, if you can.
I prize thy love more than whole mines of gold
Or all the riches that the East doth hold.
My love is such that rivers cannot quench,
Nor ought but love from thee, give recompense.
Thy love is such I can no way repay,
The heavens reward thee manifold, I pray.
Then while we live, in love let's so persèvere
That when we live no more, we may live ever.

Anne Bradsheet

The Passionate Shepherd to His Love

Come live with me, and be my love;
And we will all the pleasures prove
That hills and valleys, dales and fields,
Woods or steepy mountain yields.

And we will sit upon the rocks,
And see the shepherds feed their flocks
By shallow rivers, to whose falls
Melodious birds sing madrigals.

And I will make thee beds of roses,
And a thousand fragrant posies;
A cap of flowers, and a kirtle
Embroidered all with leaves of myrtle;

A gown made of the finest wool
Which from our pretty lambs we pull;
Fair-linèd slippers for the cold,
With buckles of the purest gold;

A belt of straw and ivy-buds,
With coral clasps and amber studs:
And if these pleasures may thee move,
Come live with me, and be my love.

The shepherd-swains shall dance and sing
For thy delight each May morning:
If these delights thy mind may move,
Then live with me, and be my love.

                              Christopher Marlowe

A Birthday

My heart is like a singing bird
   Whose nest is in a watered shoot;
My heart is like an apple-tree
   Whose boughs are bent with thick-set fruit;
My heart is like a rainbow shell
   That paddles in a halcyon sea;
My heart is gladder than all these
   Because my love is come to me.

Raise me a dais of silk and down;
   Hang it with vair and purple dyes;
Carve it in doves, and pomegranates,
   And peacocks with a hundred eyes;
Work it in gold and silver grapes,
   In leaves, and silver fleur-de-lys;
Because the birthday of my life
   Is come, my love is come to me.

Christina Rossetti

My Luve's like a Red, Red Rose

O, my Luve's like a red, red rose
    That's newly sprung in June:
O, my Luve's like the melodie
    That's sweetly played in tune!

As fair art thou, my bonnie lass,
    So deep in luve am I;
And I will luve thee still, my dear,
    Till a' the seas gang dry:

Till a' the seas gang dry, my dear,
    And the rocks melt wi' the sun;
I will luve thee still, my dear,
    While the sands o' life shall run.

And fare thee weel, my only Luve!
    And fare thee weel a while!
And I will come again, my Luve,
    Though it were ten thousand mile.

                              Robert Burns

O MISTRESS MINE

O mistress mine, where are you roaming?
O, stay and hear; your true-love's coming,
   That can sing both high and low:
Trip no further, pretty sweeting;
Journeys end in lovers' meeting,
   Every wise man's son doth know.

What is love? 'tis not hereafter;
Present mirth hath present laughter;
   What's to come is still unsure:
In delay there lies no plenty;
Then come kiss me, sweet-and-twenty,
   Youth's a stuff will not endure.

from Twelfth Night, William Shakespeare

JENNY KISSED ME

Jenny kissed me when we met,
   Jumping from the chair she sat in;
Time, you thief, who love to get
   Sweets into your list, put that in!
Say I'm weary, say I'm sad,
   Say that health and wealth have missed me,
Say I'm growing old, but add,
   Jenny kissed me.

Leigh Hunt

SONG

*S*weetest love, I do not go
    For weariness of thee,
Nor in hope the world can show
    A fitter love for me;
        But since that I
Must die at last, 'tis best,
To use my self in jest
    Thus by feigned death to die.

Yesternight the sun went hence,
    And yet is here today,
He hath no desire nor sense,
    Nor half so short a way:
        Then fear not me,
But believe that I shall make
Speedier journeys, since I take
    More wings and spurs than he.

Let not thy divining heart
    Forethink me any ill,
Destiny may take thy part,
    And may thy fears fulfil;
        But think that we
Are but turned aside to sleep;
They who one another keep
    Alive, ne'er parted be.

John Donne

SHE TELLS HER LOVE WHILE HALF ASLEEP

She tells her love while half asleep,
   In the dark hours,
      With half words whispered low:
As Earth stirs in her winter sleep
   And puts out grass and flowers
      Despite the snow,
      Despite the falling snow.

Robert Graves

SO, WE'LL GO NO MORE A-ROVING

So, we'll go no more a-roving
   So late into the night,
Though the heart be still as loving
   And the moon be still as bright.

For the sword outwears its sheath,
   And the soul wears out the breast,
And the heart must pause to breathe,
   And love itself have rest.

Though the night was made for loving,
   And the day returns too soon,
Yet we'll go no more a-roving
   By the light of the moon.

Lord Byron

Go Lovely Rose

Go lovely Rose –
Tell her, that wastes her time and me,
  That now she knows,
When I resemble her to thee,
How sweet and fair she seems to be.

  Tell her that's young,
And shuns to have her graces spied,
  That hadst thou sprung
In deserts where no men abide,
Thou must have uncommended died.

  Small is the worth
Of beauty from the light retir'd:
  Bid her come forth,
Suffer her self to be desir'd,
And not blush so to be admir'd.

  Then die, that she
The common fate of all things rare
  May read in thee,
How small a part of time they share,
That are so wondrous sweet and fair.

Edmund Waller

One Perfect Rose

A single flow'r he sent me, since we met.
 All tenderly his messenger he chose;
Deep-hearted, pure, with scented dew still wet –
 One perfect rose.

I knew the language of the floweret;
 'My fragile leaves,' it said, 'his heart enclose.'
Love long has taken for his amulet
 One perfect rose.

Why is it no one ever sent me yet
 One perfect limousine, do you suppose?
Ah no, it's always just my luck to get
 One perfect rose.

Dorothy Parker

To his Mistress's Eyes

Your eyen two will slay me suddenly:
I may the beauty of them not sustene,
So woundeth it through-out my hertĕ kene.

And but your word will healen hastily
My hertĕs woundĕ, while that it is green,
Your eyen two will slay me suddenly:
I may the beauty of them not sustene.

Upon my troth I say you faithfully,
That ye be of my life and death the queen,
For with my death the truthĕ shall be seen.
Your eyen two will slay me suddenly
I may the beauty of them not sustene,
So woundeth it through-out my hertĕ kene.

Geoffrey Chaucer

eyen: eyes

To Dianeme

Sweet, be not proud of those two eyes,
Which star-like sparkle in their skies;
Nor be you proud, that you can see
All hearts your captives, yours yet free.
Be you not proud of that rich hair,
Which wantons with the love-sick air;
Whenas that ruby which you wear,
Sunk from the tip of your soft ear,
Will last to be a precious stone
When all your world of beauty's gone.

                                    Robert Herrick

Still to be Neat

Still to be neat, still to be drest,
As you were going to a feast;
Still to be powdered, still perfumed;
Lady, it is to be presumed,
Though art's hid causes are not found,
All is not sweet, all is not sound.

Give me a look, give me a face,
That makes simplicity a grace;
Robes loosely flowing, hair as free:
Such sweet neglect more taketh me
Than all the adulteries of art;
They strike mine eyes, but not my heart.

Ben Jonson

Love Me Still

Love not me for comely grace,
For my pleasing eye or face,
  Nor for any outward part,
  No, nor for a constant heart:
    For these may fail or turn to ill,
    So thou and I shall sever:
Keep therefore a true woman's eye,
And love me still but know not why —
    So hast thou the same reason still
    To dote upon me ever!

Anonymous

Aubade

Stay, O sweet, and do not rise!
  The light that shines comes from thine eyes;
The day breaks not: it is my heart,
  Because that you and I must part.
    Stay! or else my joys will die
    And perish in their infancy.

Anonymous

Western Wind

Western wind, when wilt thou blow,
The small rain down can rain?
Christ, that my love were in my arms,
And I in my bed again!

Anonymous

Never Seek to Tell Thy Love

Never seek to tell thy love,
    Love that never told can be;
For the gentle wind does move
    Silently, invisibly.

I told my love, I told my love,
    I told her all my heart;
Trembling, cold, in ghastly fears,
    Ah, she doth depart!

Soon as she was gone from me,
    A traveller came by,
Silently, invisibly –
    He took her with a sigh.

William Blake

The Taxi

When I go away from you
The world beats dead
Like a slackened drum.
I call out for you against the jutted stars
And shout into the ridges of the wind.
Streets coming fast,
One after the other,
Wedge you away from me,
And the lamps of the city prick my eyes
So that I can no longer see your face.
Why should I leave you,
To wound myself upon the sharp edges of the night?

Amy Lowell

When I Was One-and-Twenty

When I was one-and-twenty
  I heard a wise man say,
'Give crowns and pounds and guineas
  But not your heart away;
Give pearls away and rubies
  But keep your fancy free.'
But I was one-and-twenty,
  No use to talk to me.

When I was one-and-twenty
  I heard him say again,
'The heart out of the bosom
  Was never given in vain;

'Tis paid with sighs a plenty
  And sold for endless rue.'
And I am two-and-twenty,
  And oh, 'tis true, 'tis true.

           A. E. Housman

ROSE AYLMER

*A*h, what avails the sceptred race!
　　Ah, what the form divine!
What every virtue, every grace!
　　Rose Aylmer, all were thine.

Rose Aylmer, whom these wakeful eyes
　　May weep, but never see,
A night of memories and sighs
　　I consecrate to thee.

Walter Savage Landor

LORD RANDAL

'O where hae ye been, Lord Randal, my son?
O where hae ye been, my handsome young man?'
'I hae been to the wild wood; mother, make my bed soon,
For I'm weary wi' hunting, and fain wald lie down.'

'Where gat ye your dinner, Lord Randal, my son?
Where gat ye your dinner, my handsome young man?'
'I dined wi' my true-love; mother, make my bed soon,
For I'm weary wi' hunting, and fain wald lie down.'

'What gat ye to your dinner, Lord Randal, my son?
What gat ye to your dinner, my handsome young man?'
'I gat eels boiled in broth; mother, make my bed soon,
For I'm weary wi' hunting, and fain wald lie down.'

'What became of your bloodhounds, Lord Randal, my son?
What became of your bloodhounds, my handsome young
    man?'
'O they swelled and they died; mother, make my bed soon,
For I'm weary wi' hunting, and fain wald lie down.'

'O I fear ye are poisoned, Lord Randal, my son!
O I fear ye are poisoned, my handsome young man!'
'O yes! I am poisoned; mother, make my bed soon,
For I'm sick at the heart and I fain wald lie down.'

Anonymous

Since There's No Help

Since there's no help, come let us kiss and part;
Nay, I have done, you get no more of me;
And I am glad, yea glad with all my heart,
That thus so cleanly I myself can free;
Shake hands for ever, cancel all our vows,
And when we meet at any time again,
Be it not seen in either of our brows
That we one jot of former love retain.
Now at the last gasp of love's latest breath,
When, his pulse failing, passion speechless lies,
When faith is kneeling by his bed of death,
And innocence is closing up his eyes,
    Now if thou would'st, when all have given him over,
    From death to life thou might'st him yet recover.

Michael Drayton

THE UNQUIET GRAVE

The wind doth blow to-day, my love,
    And a few small drops of rain;
I never had but one true love,
    In cold grave she was lain.

'I'll do as much for my true love
    As any young man may;
I'll sit and mourn all at her grave
    For a twelvemonth and a day.'

The twelvemonth and a day being up,
    The dead began to speak:
'Oh who sits weeping on my grave,
    And will not let me sleep?'

''Tis I, my love, sits on your grave,
    And will not let you sleep;
For I crave one kiss of your clay-cold lips,
    And that is all I seek.'

'You crave one kiss of my clay-cold lips;
    But my breath smells earthy strong;
If you have one kiss of my clay-cold lips,
    Your time will not be long.

''Tis down in yonder garden green,
   Love, where we used to walk,
The finest flower that ere was seen
   Is withered to a stalk.

'The stalk is withered dry, my love,
   So will our hearts decay;
So make yourself content, my love,
   Till God calls you away.'

                  Anonymous

I Loved a Lass

I loved a lass, a fair one,
　　As fair as e'er was seen;
She was indeed a rare one,
　　Another Sheba queen.
But, fool as then I was,
　　I thought she loved me too,
But now, alas, she's left me,
　　Falero, lero, loo.

Her hair like gold did glister,
　　Each eye was like a star;
She did surpass her sister,
　　Which passed all others far.
She would me 'honey' call,
　　She'd, O! she'd kiss me too;
But now, alas, she's left me,
　　Falero, lero, loo . . .

Her cheeks were like the cherry,
　　Her skin as white as snow;
When she was blithe and merry,
　　She angel-like did show.
Her waist exceeding small,
　　The fives did fit her shoe;
But now, alas, she's left me,
　　Falero, lero, loo . . .

Like doves we would be billing,
   And clip and kiss so fast,
Yet she would be unwilling
   That I should kiss the last;
They're Juda's kisses now,
   Since that they proved untrue.
For now, alas, she's left me,
   Falero, lero, loo.

To maidens' vows and swearing
   Henceforth no credit give,
You may give them the hearing
   But never them believe.
They are as false as fair,
   Unconstant, frail, untrue;
For mine, alas, has left me,
   Falero, lero, loo . . .

George Wither

Oh, When I Was in Love with You

Oh, when I was in love with you,
　　Then I was clean and brave,
And miles around the wonder grew,
　　How well did I behave.

And now the fancy passes by,
　　And nothing will remain,
And miles around they'll say that I
　　Am quite myself again.

　　　　　　A. E. Housman

Why So Pale and Wan?

Why so pale and wan, fond lover?
  Prythee, why so pale?
Will, when looking well can't move her,
  Looking ill prevail?
  Prythee, why so pale?

Why so dull and mute, young sinner?
  Prythee, why so mute?
Will, when speaking well can't win her,
  Saying nothing do't?
  Prythee, why so mute?

Quit, quit, for shame! this will not move,
  This cannot take her.
If of herself she will not love,
  Nothing can make her:
  The devil take her!

Sir John Suckling

LOVE AND POETRY

O Love, how thou art tired out with rhyme!
Thou art a tree whereon all poets climb;
And from thy branches everyone takes some
Of thy sweet fruit, which Fancy feeds upon.
But now thy tree is left so bare and poor,
That they can scarely gather one plum more.

Margaret, Duchess of Newcastle

SONG AND DANCE

Introduction to 'S<small>ONGS OF</small> I<small>NNOCENCE</small>'

*P*iping down the valleys wild,
    Piping songs of pleasant glee,
On a cloud I saw a child,
    And he laughing said to me:

'Pipe a song about a Lamb!'
    So I piped with merry cheer.
'Piper, pipe that song again';
    So I piped: he wept to hear.

'Drop thy pipe, thy happy pipe;
    Sing thy songs of happy cheer':
So I sang the same again,
    While he wept with joy to hear.

'Piper, sit thee down and write
    In a book, that all may read.'
So he vanished from my sight,
    And I plucked a hollow reed,

And I made a rural pen,
    And I stained the water clear,
And I wrote my happy songs
    Every child may joy to hear.

William Blake

THE SOLITARY REAPER

Behold her, single in the field,
Yon solitary Highland Lass!
Reaping and singing by herself;
Stop here, or gently pass!
Alone she cuts and binds the grain,
And sings a melancholy strain;
O listen! for the Vale profound
Is overflowing with the sound.

No Nightingale did ever chaunt
More welcome notes to weary bands
Of travellers in some shady haunt,
Among Arabian sands:
A voice so thrilling ne'er was heard
In spring-time from the Cuckoo-bird,
Breaking the silence of the seas
Among the farthest Hebrides.

Will no one tell me what she sings? –
Perhaps the plaintive numbers flow
For old, unhappy, far-off things,
And battles long ago:
Or is it some more humble lay,
Familiar matter of to-day?
Some natural sorrow, loss, or pain,
That has been, and may be again?

Whate'er the theme, the Maiden sang
As if her song could have no ending;
I saw her singing at her work,
And o'er the sickle bending; –
I listened, motionless and still;
And, as I mounted up the hill,
The music in my heart I bore,
Long after it was heard no more.

William Wordsworth

ORPHEUS WITH HIS LUTE

Orpheus with his lute made trees,
And the mountain-tops that freeze,
    Bow themselves when he did sing.
To his music plants and flowers
Ever sprung, as sun and showers
    There had made a lasting spring.

Everything that heard him play,
Even the billows of the sea,
    Hung their heads, and then lay by.
In sweet music is such art,
Killing care and grief of heart
    Fall asleep, or hearing die.

John Fletcher

THE RIVALS

I heard a bird at dawn
   Singing sweetly on a tree,
That the dew was on the lawn,
   And the wind was on the lea!
But I didn't listen to him,
   For he didn't sing to me!

I didn't listen to him,
   For he didn't sing to me
That the dew was on the lawn,
   And the wind was on the lea!
I was singing at the time
   Just as prettily as he!

I was singing all the time,
   Just as prettily as he,
About the dew upon the lawn,
   And the wind upon the lea!
So I didn't listen to him
   As he sang upon a tree!

James Stephens

Skye Boat Song

Sing me a song of a lad that is gone,
　　Say, could that lad be I?
Merry of soul he sailed on a day
　　Over the sea to Skye.

Mull was astern, Rum on the port,
　　Eigg on the starboard bow;
Glory of youth glowed in his soul:
　　Where is that glory now?

Sing me a song of a lad that is gone,
　　Say, could that lad be I?
Merry of soul he sailed on a day
　　Over the sea to Skye.

Give me again all that was there,
　　Give me the sun that shone!
Give me the eyes, give me the soul,
　　Give me the lad that's gone!

Sing me a song of a lad that is gone,
　　Say, could that lad be I?
Merry of soul he sailed on a day
　　Over the sea to Skye.

Billow and breeze, islands and seas,
　　Mountains of rain and sun,
All that was good, all that was fair,
　　All that was me is gone.

Robert Louis Stevenson

A SMUGGLER'S SONG

*I*f you wake at midnight, and hear a horse's feet,
Don't go drawing back the blind, or looking in the street,
Them that ask no questions isn't told a lie.
Watch the wall, my darling, while the Gentlemen go by!
   Five and twenty ponies,
   Trotting through the dark –
   Brandy for the Parson,
   'Baccy for the Clerk;
   Laces for a lady, letters for a spy,
And watch the wall, my darling, while the Gentlemen go by!

Running round the woodlump if you chance to find
Little barrels, roped and tarred, all full of brandy-wine,
Don't you shout to come and look, nor use 'em for your play.
Put the brishwood back again – and they'll be gone next day!

If you see the stable-door setting open wide;
If you see a tired horse lying down inside;
If your mother mends a coat cut about and tore;
If the lining's wet and warm – don't you ask no more!

If you meet King George's men, dressed in blue and red,
You be careful what you say, and mindful what is said.
If they call you 'pretty maid,' and chuck you 'neath the chin,
Don't you tell where no one is, nor yet where no one's been!

Knocks and footsteps round the house – whistles after dark –
You've no call for running out till the house-dogs bark.
Trusty's here, and *Pincher*'s here, and see how dumb they lie –
They don't fret to follow when the Gentlemen go by!

If you do as you've been told, 'likely there's a chance,
You'll be give a dainty doll, all the way from France,
With a cap of Valenciennes, and a velvet hood –
A present from the Gentlemen, along o' being good!
        Five and twenty ponies,
        Trotting through the dark –
        Brandy for the Parson,
        'Baccy for the Clerk.
Them that asks no questions isn't told a lie –
Watch the wall, my darling, while the Gentlemen go by!

Rudyard Kipling

EVERYONE SANG

*E*veryone suddenly burst out singing;
And I was filled with such delight
As prisoned birds must find in freedom
Winging wildly across the white
Orchards and dark green fields; on; on; and out of sight.

Everyone's voice was suddenly lifted,
And beauty came like the setting sun.
My heart was shaken with tears, and horror
Drifted away . . . O, but every one
Was a bird; and the song was wordless; the singing will
    never be done.

Siegfried Sassoon

THE SINGING CAT

*I*t was a little captive cat
    Upon a crowded train
His mistress takes him from his box
    To ease his fretful pain.

She holds him tight upon her knee
    The graceful animal
And all the people look at him
    He is so beautiful.
But oh he pricks and oh he prods
    And turns upon her knee
Then lifteth up his innocent voice
    In plaintive melody.

He lifteth up his innocent voice
    He lifteth up, he singeth
And to each human countenance
    A smile of grace he bringeth.

He lifteth up his innocent paw
    Upon her breast he clingeth
And everybody cries, Behold
    The cat, the cat that singeth.

His lifteth up his innocent voice
    He lifteth up, he singeth
And all the people warm themselves
    In the love his beauty bringeth.

                    Stevie Smith

Night Song

On moony nights the dogs bark shrill
Down the valley and up the hill.

There's one who is angry to behold
The moon so unafraid and cold,
That makes the earth as bright as day,
But yet unhappy, dead, and grey.

Another in his strawy lair,
Says: 'Who's a-howling over there?
By heavens I will stop him soon
From interfering with the moon.'

So back he barks, with throat upthrown;
'You leave our moon, our moon alone.'
And other distant dogs respond
Beyond the fields, beyond, beyond.

                              Frances Cornford

WALTZING MATILDA

Once a jolly swagman camped by a billabong
    Under the shade of a coolibah tree,
And he sang as he watched and waited till his billy boiled,
    'You'll come a-waltzing Matilda with me!'
Waltzing Matilda, waltzing Matilda,
    You'll come a-waltzing Matilda with me:
And he sang as he watched and waited till his billy boiled,
    'You'll come a-waltzing Matilda with me!'

Down came a jumbuck to drink at the billabong,
    Up jumped the swagman and grabbed him with glee,
And he sang as he stowed that jumbuck in his tucker bag,
    'You'll come a-waltzing Matilda with me!'
Waltzing Matilda, waltzing Matilda
    You'll come a-waltzing Matilda with me:
And he sang as he stowed that jumbuck in his tucker bag,
    'You'll come a-waltzing Matilda with me!'

Up rode the squatter mounted on his thoroughbred,
    Up rode the troopers, one, two, three.
'Where's that jolly jumbuck you've got in your tucker bag?
    You'll come a-waltzing Matilda with me!'
Waltzing Matilda, waltzing Matilda,
    You'll come a-waltzing Matilda with me:
'Where's that jolly jumbuck you've got in your tucker bag?
    You'll come a-waltzing Matilda with me!'

Up jumped the swagman and sprang into the billabong,
    'You'll never take me alive!' said he.
And his ghost may be heard as you pass by that billabong,
    'You'll never take me alive!' said he.
Waltzing Matilda, waltzing Matilda,
    You'll come a-waltzing Matilda with me,
And his ghost may be heard as you pass by that billabong,
    'You'll come a-waltzing Matilda with me!'

                    Andrew Barton Paterson

Waltzing Matilda: to tramp about countryside carrying swag
swagman: casual worker
billabong: stagnant pool
billy: kettle used in camp cooking
jumbuck: sheep
tucker: food
squatter: sheep-farmer

Is't Not Fine to Dance and Sing?

*H*ey nonny no!
Men are fools that wish to die!
Is't not fine to dance and sing
When the bells of death do ring?
Is't not fine to swim in wine,
And turn upon the toe
And sing hey nonny no,
When the winds do blow,
And the seas do flow?
Hey nonny no!

Anonymous

SONG

Shake off your heavy trance,
　　And leap into a dance,
Such as no mortals use to tread:
　　Fit only for Apollo
To play to, for the moon to lead,
　　And all the stars to follow.

Francis Beaumont

A PIPER

A piper in the streets today
Set up and tuned, and started to play,
And away, away, away on the tide
Of his music we started; on every side
Doors and windows were opened wide,
And men left down their work and came,
And women with petticoats coloured like flame
And little bare feet that were blue with cold,
Went dancing back to the age of gold,
And all the world went gay, went gay,
For half an hour in the street today.

Seumas O'Sullivan

The Fiddler of Dooney

When I play on my fiddle in Dooney,
Folk dance like a wave of the sea;
My cousin is priest in Kilvarnet,
My brother in Mocharabuiee.

I passed my brother and cousin:
They read in their books of prayer;
I read in my books of songs
I bought at the Sligo fair.

When we come at the end of time
To Peter sitting in state,
He will smile on the three old spirits,
But call me first through the gate;

For the good are always the merry,
Save by an evil chance,
And the merry love the fiddle,
And the merry love to dance:

And when the folk there spy me,
They will all come up to me,
With 'Here is the fiddler of Dooney!'
And dance like a wave of the sea.

William Butler Yeats

On her Dancing

I stood and saw my mistress dance,
      Silent, and with so fixed an eye,
Some might suppose me in a trance.
      But being askèd why,
By one that knew I was in love,
      I could not but impart
My wonder, to behold her move
So nimbly with a marble heart.

James Shirley

TARANTELLA

*D*o you remember an Inn,
Miranda?
Do you remember an Inn?
And the tedding and the spreading
Of the straw for a bedding,
And the fleas that tease in the High Pyrenees,
And the wine that tasted of the tar,
And the cheers and the jeers of the young muleteers
(Under the vine of the dark verandah)?
Do you remember an Inn,
Miranda?
Do you remember an Inn?
And the cheers and the jeers of the young muleteers
Who hadn't got a penny,
And who weren't paying any,
And the hammer at the doors and the Din?

And the Hip! Hop! Hap!
Of the clap
Of the hands to the twirl and the swirl
Of the girl gone chancing,
Glancing,
Dancing,
Backing and advancing,
Snapping of the clapper to the spin
Out and in —
And the Ting, Tong, Tang of the Guitar!
Do you remember an Inn,
Miranda?
Do you remember an Inn?

Never more,
Miranda,
Never more.
Only the high peaks hoar:
And Aragon a torrent at the door.
No sound
In the walls of the Halls where falls
The tread
Of the feet of the dead to the ground,
No sound:
But the boom
Of the far Waterfall like Doom.

                              Hilaire Belloc

My Papa's Waltz

The whisky on your breath
Could make a small boy dizzy;
But I hung on like death:
Such waltzing was not easy.

We romped until the pans
Slid from the kitchen shelf;
My mother's countenance
Could not unfrown itself.

The hand that held my wrist
Was battered on one knuckle;
At every step you missed
My right ear scraped a buckle.

You beat time on my head
With a palm caked hard by dirt,
Then waltzed me off to bed
Still clinging to your shirt.

                    Theodore Roethke

My Mother Saw a Dancing Bear

My mother saw a dancing bear
By the schoolyard, a day in June.
The keeper stood with chain and bar
And whistle-pipe, and played a tune.

And Bruin lifted up its head
And lifted up its dusty feet,
And all the children laughed to see
It caper in the summer heat.

They watched as for the Queen it died.
They watched it march. They watched it halt.
They heard the keeper as he cried,
'Now, roly-poly!' 'Somersault!'

And then, my mother said, there came
The keeper with a begging-cup,
The bear with burning coat of fur,
Shaming the laughter to a stop.

They paid a penny for the dance,
But what they saw was not the show;
Only, in Bruin's aching eyes,
Far-distant forests, and the snow.

Charles Causley

PEOPLE

LINEAGE

My grandmothers were strong.
They followed plows and bent to toil.
They moved through fields sowing seed.
They touched earth and grain grew.
They were full of sturdiness and singing.
My grandmothers were strong.

My grandmothers are full of memories
Smelling of soap and onions and wet clay
With veins rolling roughly over quick hands
They have many clean words to say.
My grandmothers were strong.
Why am I not as they?

Margaret Walker

MORNING SONG

Love set you going like a fat gold watch.
The midwife slapped your footsoles, and your bald cry
Took its place among the elements.

Our voices echo, magnifying your arrival. New statue
In a drafty museum, your nakedness
Shadows our safety. We stand round blankly as walls.

I'm no more your mother
Than the cloud that distils a mirror to reflect its own slow
Effacement at the wind's hand.

All night your moth-breath
Flickers among the flat pink roses. I wake to listen:
A far sea moves in my ear.

One cry, and I stumble from bed, cow-heavy and floral
In my Victorian nightgown.
Your mouth opens clean as a cat's. The window square

Whitens and swallows its dull stars. And now you try
Your handful of notes:
The clear vowels rise like balloons.

                                        Sylvia Plath

The Chimney Sweeper

When my mother died I was very young,
And my father sold me while yet my tongue
Could scarcely cry ' 'weep! 'weep! 'weep! 'weep!'
So your chimneys I sweep, and in soot I sleep.

There's little Tom Dacre, who cried when his head,
That curled like a lamb's back, was shaved: so I said
'Hush, Tom! never mind it, for when your head's bare
You know that the soot cannot spoil your white hair.'

And so he was quiet, and that very night,
As Tom was a-sleeping, he had such a sight!
That thousands of sweepers, Dick, Joe, Ned, and Jack,
Were all of them locked up in coffins of black.
And by came an Angel who had a bright key,
And he opened the coffins and set them all free;
Then down a green plain leaping, laughing, they run,
And wash in a river, and shine in the Sun.

Then naked and white, all their bags left behind,
They rise upon clouds and sport in the wind;
And the Angel told Tom, if he'd be a good boy,
He'd have God for his father, and never want joy.

And so Tom awoke; and we rose in the dark,
And got with our bags and our brushes to work.
Tho' the morning was cold, Tom was happy and warm;
So if all do their duty they need not fear harm.

William Blake

THE COUNTRY LAD

Who can live in heart so glad
　As the merry country lad?

Who upon a fair green balk
May at pleasure sit and talk,
　　And amid the azure skies
　　See the morning sun arise,
While he hears in every spring
How the birds do chirp and sing:
　　Or before the hounds in cry
　　See the hare go stealing by:
Or along the shallow brook,
Angling with a baited hook,
See the fishes leap and play
In a blessëd sunny day:
　　Or to hear the partridge call
　　Till she have her covey all:
Or to see the subtle fox,
How the villain plies the box;
After feeding on his prey,
How he closely sneaks away,

Through the hedge and down the furrow
Till he gets into his burrow:
  Then the bee to gather honey;
  And the little black-haired coney,
  On a bank for sunny place,
  With her forefeet wash her face:
Are not these, with thousands moe
Than the courts of kings do know,
The true pleasing spirit's sights
That may breed true love's delights?

Nicholas Breton

balk: bank
covey: brood
plies the box: raids the chicken run

SALLY

She was a dog-rose kind of girl:
elusive, scattery as petals;
scratchy sometimes, tripping you like briars.
She teased the boys
turning this way and that, not to be tamed
or taught any more than the wind.
Even in school the word 'ought'
had no meaning for Sally.
On dull days
she'd sit quiet as a mole at her desk
delving in thought.
But when the sun called
she was gone, running the blue day down
till the warm hedgerows prickled the dusk
and moths flickered out.

Her mother scolded; Dad
gave her the hazel-switch,
said her head was stuffed with feathers
and a starling tongue.
But they couldn't take the shine out of her.
Even when it rained
you felt the sun saved under her skin.
She'd a way of escape
laughing at you from the bright end of a tunnel,
leaving you in the dark.

Phoebe Hesketh

STREET BOY

*J*ust you look at me, man,
Stompin' down the street
My crombie's stuffed with biceps
My boots is filled with feet.

Just you hark to me, man,
When they call us out
My head is full of silence
My mouth is full of shout.

Just you watch me move, man,
Steady like a clock
My heart is spaced on blue beat
My soul is toned on rock.

Just you read my name, man,
Writ for all to see
The walls is red with stories
The streets is filled with me.

Gareth Owen

MEG MERRILIES

Old Meg she was a gipsy;
 And lived upon the moors:
Her bed it was the brown heath turf,
 And her house was out of doors.
Her apples were swart blackberries,
 Her currants, pods o' broom;
Her wine was dew of the wild white rose,
 Her book a churchyard tomb.

Her brothers were the craggy hills,
 Her sisters larchen trees;
Alone with her great family
 She lived as she did please.
No breakfast had she many a morn,
 No dinner many a noon,
And, 'stead of supper, she would stare
 Full hard against the moon.

But every morn, of woodbine fresh
 She made her garlanding,
And, every night, the dark yew glen
 She wove, and she would sing.
And with her fingers, old and brown,
 She plaited mats of rushes,
And gave them to the cottagers
 She met among the bushes.

Old Meg was brave as Margaret Queen,
    And tall as Amazon;
An old red blanket cloak she wore,
    A chip-hat had she on:
God rest her aged bones somewhere!
    She died full long agone.

John Keats

Farm Child

Look at this village boy, his head is stuffed
    With all the nests he knows, his pockets with flowers,
    Snail-shells and bits of glass, the fruit of hours
Spent in the fields by thorn and thistle tuft.
Look at his eyes, see the harebell hiding there;
    Mark how the sun has freckled his smooth face
Like a finch's egg under that bush of hair
    That dares the wind, and in the mixen now
    Notice his poise; from such unconscious grace
    Earth breeds and beckons to the stubborn plough.

R. S. Thomas

THE MILLERE

*T*he Millere was a stout carl for the nones;
Full byg he was of brawn, and eek of bones.
That proved wel, for over al ther he cam,
At wrastlynge he wolde have alwey the ram.
He was short-sholdred, brood, a thikkè knarre;
Ther was no dore that he nolde heve of harre,
Or breke it at a rennying with his heed.
His berd as any sowe or fox was reed,
And therto brood, as though it were a spade.
Upon the cop right of his nose he hade
A werte, and theron stood a toft of herys,
Reed as the brustles of a sowès erys;
His nosèthirlès blakè were and wyde.
A swerd and bokeler bar he by his syde.
His mouth as greet was as a greet forneys.
He was a janglere and a goliardeys,
And that was moost of synne and harlotries.
Wel koude he stelen corn and tollen thries;
And yet he hadde a thombe of gold, pardee.
A whit cote and a blew hood werèd he.
A baggèpipe well koude he blowe and sowne,
And therwithal he broghte us out of towne.

Geoffrey Chaucer

THE MILLER

A strong chap was the miller, truth to tell,
Bulging with muscles, and big-boned as well.
So, when it came to wrestling, his great size
Always ensured he walked off with first prize;
Short-shouldered, broad and brawny he could wrench free
A stout door from its hinges, casually,
Or smash it down, ramming it with his head.
Just like a sow or fox, his beard was red
And broad, besides – in shape a perfect spade.
His nose, right at its very tip, displayed
A wart from which there grew a tuft of hairs
As red as bristles in an old sow's ears;
Meanwhile, his nostrils were both black and wide.
He bore a sword and buckler at his side.
His mouth was massive as a furnace door.
He'd talk loud-mouthed about his sins and roar
With laughter at his own lewd wantonness,
Bragging of all his shameful wickedness.
With his gold thumb he stole corn, and well knew
How to make clients pay three times their due.
In white coat and blue hood, he marched us all
Out of the town, to his shrill bagpipes' squall.

Modern version by Raymond Wilson

To Mistress Margaret Hussey

Merry Màrgarèt
As midsummer flower,
Gentle as falcon
   Or hawk of the tower:
With solace and gladness,
Much mirth and no madness,
All good and no badness;
So joyously,
So maidenly,
So womanly
Her demeaning
In every thing,
Far, far passing
That I can endite,
Or suffice to write
Of merry Màrgarèt
   As midsummer flower,
Gentle as falcon
   Or hawk of the tower.

As patient and still
And as full of good will
As fair Isaphill,
Coliander,
Sweet pomander,
Good Cassander;
Steadfast of thought,
Well made, well wrought,
Far may be sought
Erst that ye can find
So courteous, so kind
As merry Màrgarèt,
   This midsummer flower,
Gentle as falcon
   Or hawk of the tower.

John Skelton

gentle: noble
coliander: aromatic seed
pomander: aromatic ball
erst that: before

BLIND POET

*T*hus with the year
Seasons return; but not to me returns
Day, or the sweet approach of even or morn,
Or sight of vernal bloom, or summer's rose
Or flocks, or herds, or human face divine;
But cloud instead and ever-during dark
Surrounds me, from the cheerful ways of men
Cut off, and, for the book of knowledge fair,
Presented with a universal blank
Of Nature's works, to me expunged and rased,
And wisdom at one entrance quite shut out.
So much the rather thou, Celestial Light,
Shine inward, and the mind through all her powers
Irradiate; there plant eyes; all mist from thence
Purge and disperse, that I may see and tell
Of things invisible to mortal sight.

from Paradise Lost, Book 3, John Milton

PETER GRIMES

*W*ith greedy eye he looked on all he saw;
He knew not justice, and he laughed at law;
On all he marked he stretched his ready hand;
He fished by water, and he filched on land.
Oft in the night has Peter dropped his oar,
Fled from his boat and sought for prey on shore;
Oft up the hedge-row glided, on his back
Bearing the orchard's produce in a sack,
Or farm-yard load, tugged fiercely from the stack;
And as these wrongs to greater numbers rose,
The more he looked on all men as his foes.
   He built a mud-walled hovel, where he kept
His various wealth, and there he oft-times slept . . .

from Peter Grimes, George Crabbe

PROUD MAISIE

Proud Maisie is in the wood,
   Walking so early;
Sweet Robin sits on the bush,
   Singing so rarely.

'Tell me, thou bonny bird,
   When shall I marry me?'
– 'When six braw gentlemen
   Kirkward shall carry ye.'

'Who makes the bridal bed,
   Birdie, say truly?'
– 'The grey-headed sexton
   That delves the grave duly.
'The glow-worm o'er grave and stone
   Shall light thee steady;
The owl from the steeple sing
   Welcome, proud lady!'

                              Sir Walter Scott

Abou Ben Adhem

Abou Ben Adhem (may his tribe increase)
Awoke one night from a deep dream of peace,
And saw within the moonlight in his room,
Making it rich and like a lily in bloom,
An Angel writing in a book of gold: –
Exceeding peace had made Ben Adhem bold,
And to the Presence in the room, he said,
'What writest thou?' The Vision raised its head,
And with a look made of all sweet accord,
Answered, 'The names of those who love the Lord.'
'And is mine one?' said Abou. 'Nay, not so,'
Replied the Angel. Abou spoke more low,
But cheerly still; and said, 'I pray thee then,
Write me as one that loves his fellow-men.'

The Angel wrote and vanished. The next night
It came again with a great wakening light,
And showed the names whom love of God had blessed,
And lo! Ben Adhem's name led all the rest.

Leigh Hunt

MY GRANDMOTHER

She kept an antique shop – or it kept her.
Among Apostle spoons and Bristol glass,
The faded silks, the heavy furniture,
She watched her own reflection in the brass
Salvers and silver bowls, as if to prove
Polish was all, there was no need of love.

And I remember how I once refused
To go out with her, since I was afraid.
It was perhaps a wish not to be used
Like antique objects. Though she never said
That she was hurt, I still could feel the guilt
Of that refusal, guessing how she felt.

Later, too frail to keep a shop, she put
All her best things in one long narrow room.
The place smelt old, of things too long kept shut.
The smell of absences where shadows come
That can't be polished. There was nothing then
To give her own reflection back again.

And when she died I felt no grief at all,
Only the guilt of what I once refused.
I walked into her room among the tall
Sideboards and cupboards – things she never used
But needed: and no finger-marks were there,
Only the new dust falling through the air.

                                        Elizabeth Jennings

CHILDHOOD

I used to think that grown-up people chose
To have stiff backs and wrinkles round their nose
And veins like small fat snakes on either hand,
On purpose to be grand,
Till through the banisters I watched one day
My great-aunt Etty's friend who was going away,
And how her onyx beads had come unstrung,
I saw her grope to find them as they rolled;
And then I knew that she was helplessly old,
As I was helplessly young.

Frances Cornford

Written in Northampton County Asylum

I am: yet what I am none cares or knows.
     My friends forsake me like a memory lost;
I am the self-consumer of my woes,
     They rise and vanish in oblivious host,
Like shades in love and death's oblivion lost;
And yet I am, and live with shadows tossed

Into the nothingness of scorn and noise,
     Into the living sea of waking dreams,
Where there is neither sense of life nor joys,
     But the vast shipwreck of my life's esteems;
And e'en the dearest, that I loved the best,
Are strange – nay, rather stranger than the rest.

I long for scenes where man has never trod,
     A place where woman never smiled or wept;
There to abide with my Creator, God,
     And sleep as I in childhood sweetly slept:
Untroubling and untroubled where I lie,
The grass below – above, the vaulted sky.

                                        John Clare

from I AM THE ONE

I am the one whom ringdoves see
     Through chinks in boughs
     When they do not rouse
     In sudden dread,
But stay on cooing, as if they said:
     'Oh; it's only he.'

I am the passer when up-eared hares,
     Stirred as they eat
     The new-sprung wheat,
     Their munch resume
As if they thought: 'He is one for whom
     Nobody cares.'

             Thomas Hardy

FIGURES OF FUN

You Are Old, Father William

'You are old, Father William,' the young man said,
  'And your hair has become very white;
And yet you incessantly stand on your head –
  Do you think, at your age, it is right?'

'In my youth,' Father William replied to his son,
  'I feared it might injure the brain;
But, now that I'm perfectly sure I have none,
  Why, I do it again and again.'

'You are old,' said the youth, 'as I mentioned before,
  And have grown most uncommonly fat;
Yet you turned a back-somersault in at the door –
  Pray, what is the reason for that?'

'In my youth,' said the sage, as he shook his grey locks,
  'I kept all my limbs very supple
By the use of this ointment – one shilling the box –
  Allow me to sell you a couple?'

'You are old,' said the youth, 'and your jaws are too weak
  For anything tougher than suet;
Yet you finished the goose, with the bones and the beak –
  Pray, how did you manage to do it?'

'In my youth,' said his father, 'I took to the law,
  And argued each case with my wife;
And the muscular strength, which it gave to my jaw,
  Has lasted the rest of my life.'

'You are old,' said the youth, 'one would hardly suppose
    That your eye was as steady as ever;
Yet you balanced an eel on the end of your nose –
    What made you so awfully clever?'

'I have answered three questions, and that is enough,'
    Said his father. 'Don't give yourself airs!
Do you think I can listen all day to such stuff?
    Be off, or I'll kick you downstairs!'

                                                 Lewis Carroll

Matilda
who told lies, and was burned to death

Matilda told such Dreadful Lies,
It made one Gasp and Stretch one's Eyes;
Her Aunt, who from her Earliest Youth,
Had kept a Strict Regard for Truth,
Attempted to Believe Matilda:
The effort very nearly killed her,
And would have done so, had not She
Discovered this Infirmity.
For once, towards the Close of Day,
Matilda, growing tired of play,
And finding she was left alone,
Went tiptoe to the Telephone
And summoned the Immediate Aid
Of London's Noble Fire-Brigade.

Within an hour the Gallant Band
Were pouring in on every hand,
From Putney, Hackney Downs and Bow.
With Courage high and Hearts a-glow,
They galloped, roaring through the Town,
'Matilda's House is Burning Down!'
Inspired by British Cheers and Loud
Proceeding from the Frenzied Crowd,
They ran their ladders through a score
Of windows on the Ball Room Floor;
And took Peculiar Pains to Souse
The Pictures up and down the House,
Until Matilda's Aunt succeeded
In showing them they were not needed;

And even then she had to pay
To get the Men to go away!
It happened that a few Weeks later
Her Aunt was off to the Theatre
To see that Interesting Play
The Second Mrs Tanqueray.
She had refused to take her Niece
To hear that Entertaining Piece:
A Deprivation Just and Wise
To Punish her for Telling Lies.
That Night a Fire DID break out –
You should have heard Matilda Shout!
You should have heard her Scream and Bawl,
And throw the window up and call
To People passing in the Street –
(The rapidly increasing Heat
Encouraging her to obtain
Their confidence) – but all in vain!
For every time She shouted 'Fire!'
They only answered 'Little Liar!'
And therefore when her Aunt returned,
Matilda, and the House, were Burned.

Hilaire Belloc

Henry King

*T*he Chief Defect of Henry King
Was chewing little bits of String.
At last he swallowed some which tied
Itself in ugly Knots inside.
Physicians of the Utmost Fame
Were called at once; but when they came
They answered, as they took their Fees,
'There is no Cure for this Disease.
Henry will very soon be dead.'
His parents stood about his Bed
Lamenting his Untimely Death,
When Henry, with his Latest Breath
Cried, 'Oh, my Friends, be warned by me,
That Breakfast, Dinner, Lunch and Tea
Are all the Human Frame requires . . .'
With that, the Wretched Child expires.

Hilaire Belloc

MY SISTER JANE

*A*nd I say nothing – no, not a word
About our Jane. Haven't you heard
She's a bird, a bird, a bird, a bird.
Oh it never would do to let folks know
My sister's nothing but a great big crow.

Each day (we daren't send her to school)
She pulls on stockings of thick blue wool
To make her pin crow legs look right,
Then fits a wig of curls on tight,
And dark spectacles – a huge pair
To cover her very crowy stare.
Oh it never would do to let folks know
My sister's nothing but a great big crow.

When visitors come she sits upright
(With her wings and her tail tucked out of sight).
They think her queer but extremely polite.
Then when the visitors have gone
She whips out her wings and with her wig on
Whirls through the house at the height of your head –
Duck, duck, or she'll knock you dead.
Oh it never would do to let folks know
My sister's nothing but a great big crow.

At meals whatever she sees she'll stab it —
Because she's a crow and that's a crow habit.
My mother says, 'Jane! Your manners! Please!'
Then she'll sit quietly on the cheese,
Or play the piano nicely by dancing on the keys —
Oh it never would do to let folks know
My sister's nothing but a great big crow.

Ted Hughes

QUIET FUN

My son Augustus, in the street, one day,
   Was feeling quite exceptionally merry.
A stranger asked him: 'Can you tell me, pray,
   The quickest way to Brompton Cemetery?'
'The quickest way? You bet I can!' said Gus,
And pushed the fellow underneath a bus.

*   *   *

Whatever people say about my son,
He does enjoy his little bit of fun.

Harry Graham

SIR SMASHUM UPPE

Good afternoon, Sir Smashum Uppe!
We're having tea: do take a cup!
Sugar and milk? Now let me see –
Two lumps, I think? . . . Good gracious me!
The silly thing slipped off your knee!
Pray don't apologize, old chap:
A very trivial mishap!
So clumsy of you? How absurd!
My dear Sir Smashum, not a word!
Now do sit down and have another,
And tell us all about your brother –
You know, the one who broke his head.
Is the poor fellow still in bed?
A chair – allow me, sir! . . . Great Scott!
That *was* a nasty smash! Eh, what?
Oh, not at all: the chair was old –
Queen Anne, or so we have been told.
We've got at least a dozen more:
Just leave the pieces on the floor.
I want you to admire our view:
Come nearer to the window, do;
And look how beautiful . . . Tut, tut!
You didn't see that it was shut?
I hope you are not badly cut!
Not hurt? A fortunate escape!
Amazing! Not a single scrape!
And now, if you have finished tea,
I fancy you might like to see
A little thing or two I've got.
That china plate? Yes, worth a lot:
A beauty too . . . Ah, there it goes!

I trust it didn't hurt your toes?
Your elbow brushed it off the shelf?
Of course: I've done the same myself.
And now, my dear Sir Smashum – Oh,
You surely don't intend to go?
You *must* be off? Well, come again,
So glad you're fond of porcelain.

E. V. Rieu

COLONEL FAZACKERLEY

Colonel Fazackerley Butterworth-Toast
Bought an old castle complete with a ghost,
But someone or other forgot to declare
To Colonel Fazack that the spectre was there.

On the very first evening, while waiting to dine,
The Colonel was taking a fine sherry wine,
When the ghost, with a furious flash and a flare,
Shot out of the chimney and shivered, 'Beware!'

Colonel Fazackerley put down his glass
And said, 'My dear fellow, that's really first class!
I just can't conceive how you do it at all.
I imagine you're going to a Fancy Dress Ball?'

At this, the dread ghost gave a withering cry.
Said the Colonel (his monocle firm in his eye),
'Now just how you do it I wish I could think.
Do sit down and tell me, and please have a drink.'

The ghost in his phosphorous cloak gave a roar
And floated about between ceiling and floor.
He walked through a wall and returned through a pane
And backed up the chimney and came down again.

Said the Colonel, 'With laughter I'm feeling quite weak!'
(As trickles of merriment ran down his cheek).
'My house-warming party I hope you won't spurn.
You *must* say you'll come and you'll give us a turn!'

At this, the poor spectre – quite out of his wits –
Proceeded to shake himself almost to bits.
He rattled his chains and he clattered his bones
And he filled the whole castle with mumbles and moans.

But Colonel Fazackerley, just as before,
Was simply delighted and called out, 'Encore!'
At which the ghost vanished, his efforts in vain,
And never was seen at the castle again.

'Oh dear, what a pity!' said Colonel Fazack.
'I don't know his name, so I can't call him back.'
And then with a smile that was hard to define,
Colonel Fazackerley went in to dine.

                                        Charles Causley

SCHOOL

The False Knight upon the Road

'*O* where are you going?'
Quoth the false knight upon the road:
'I'm going to school.'
Quoth the wee boy, and still he stood.

'What is that upon your back?'
Quoth the false knight upon the road:
'Why, sure it is my books.'
Quoth the wee boy, and still he stood.

'What is that you've got in your arm?'
Quoth the false knight upon the road:
'Why sure it is my peat.'
Quoth the wee boy, and still he stood.

'Whose are those sheep?'
Quoth the false knight upon the road:
'They're mine and my mother's.'
Quoth the wee boy, and still he stood.

'How many of them are mine?'
Quoth the false knight upon the road:
'All them that have blue tails.'
Quoth the wee boy, and still he stood.

'I wish you were on yon tree.'
Quoth the false knight upon the road:
'And a good ladder under me.'
Quoth the wee boy, and still he stood.

peat: peat for the school fire

'And the ladder for to break.'
Quoth the false knight upon the road:
'And *you* for to fall down.'
Quoth the wee boy, and still he stood.

'I wish you were in yon sea.'
Quoth the false knight upon the road:
'And a good boat under me.'
Quoth the wee boy, and still he stood.

'And the boat for to break.'
Quoth the false knight upon the road:
'And *you* to be drowned.'
Quoth the wee boy, and still he stood.

Anonymous

A Fight at School

Upon a day of wind and heavy rain
A crowd was huddling in the porch at school:
As I came up I heard a voice cry out,
'Ho, ho! here comes the lad who talks with ghosts,
Sitting upon the graves.' They laughed and jeered,
And gathered round me in a mocking ring,
And hurt me with their faces and their eyes.
With bitter words I smote them in my hate,
As with a weapon. A sudden blow, and wrath
Sprang upward like a flame. I struck, and blood,
Brighter than rubies, gleamed upon my hand;
And at the beauteous sight, from head to heel
A tiger's joy ran tingling through my veins,
And every finger hungered for a throat.
I burst the broken ring, and darted off
With my blood boiling, and my pulses mad.
I did not feel the rain upon my face;
With burning mouth I drank the cooling wind; –
And then, as if my limbs were touched by death,
A shudder shook me, all the rage that sprang
Like sudden fire in a deserted house
Making the windows fierce, had passed away;
And the cold rain beat heavy on me now;
The winds went through me.

from A Boy's Poem, Alexander Smith

ROMANCE

When I was but thirteen or so
   I went into a golden land,
Chimborazo, Cotopaxi
   Took me by the hand.

My father died, my brother too,
   They passed like fleeting dreams.
I stood where Popocatapetl
   In the sunlight gleams.

I dimly heard the Master's voice
   And boys far-off at play,
Chimborazo, Cotopaxi
   Had stolen me away.

I walked in a great golden dream
   To and fro from school —
Shining Popocatapetl
   The dusty streets did rule.

I walked home with a gold dark boy
   And never a word I'd say,
Chimborazo, Cotopaxi
   Had taken my speech away:

I gazed entranced upon his face
  Fairer than any flower –
O shining Popocatapetl
  It was thy magic hour:

The houses, people, traffic seemed
  Thin fading dreams by day,
Chimborazo, Cotopaxi
  They had stolen my soul away!

W. J. Turner

TIMOTHY WINTERS

Timothy Winters comes to school
With eyes as wide as a football-pool,
Ears like bombs and teeth like splinters:
A blitz of a boy is Timothy Winters.
His belly is white, his neck is dark,
And his hair is an exclamation mark.
His clothes are enough to scare a crow
And through his britches the blue winds blow.

When teacher talks he won't hear a word
And he shoots down dead the arithmetic-bird,
He licks the patterns off his plate
And he's not even heard of the Welfare State.

Timothy Winters has bloody feet
And he lives in a house on Suez Street,
He sleeps in a sack on the kitchen floor
And they say there aren't boys like him any more.

Old man Winters likes his beer
And his missus ran off with a bombardier,
Grandma sits in the grate with a gin
And Timothy's dosed with an aspirin.

The Welfare Worker lies awake
But the law's as tricky as a ten-foot snake,
So Timothy Winters drinks his cup
And slowly goes on growing up.

At Morning Prayers the Headmaster helves
For children less fortunate than ourselves,
And the loudest response in the room is when
Timothy Winters roars 'Amen!'

So come one angel, come on ten:
Timothy Winters says 'Amen'
Amen amen amen amen.
Timothy Winters, Lord.
          Amen.

                    Charles Causley

My Parents Kept Me from Children who Were Rough

My parents kept me from children who were rough
And who threw words like stones and who wore torn clothes.
Their thighs showed through rags. They ran in the street
And climbed cliffs and stripped by the country streams.

I feared more than tigers their muscles like iron
And their jerking hands and their knees tight on my arms.
I feared the salt coarse pointing of those boys
Who copied my lisp behind me on the road.

They were lithe, they sprang out behind hedges
Like dogs to bark at our world. They threw mud
And I looked another way, pretending to smile.
I longed to forgive them, yet they never smiled.

Stephen Spender

The Schoolmaster

*B*eside yon straggling fence that skirts the way,
With blossomed furze unprofitably gay,
There, in his noisy mansion, skilled to rule,
The village master taught his little school;
A man severe he was, and stern to view,
I knew him well, and every truant knew;
Well had the boding tremblers learned to trace
The day's disasters in his morning face;
Full well they laughed with counterfeited glee
At all his jokes, for many a joke had he;
Full well the busy whisper, circling round,
Conveyed the dismal tidings when he frowned;
Yet he was kind, or, if severe in aught,
The love he bore to learning was in fault;
The village all declared how much he knew;
'Twas certain he could write, and cypher too;
Lands he could measure, terms and tides presage,
And even the story ran that he could gauge;
In arguing too, the parson owned his skill,
For e'en though vanquished, he could argue still;
While words of learned length and thundering sound
Amazed the gazing rustics ranged around,
And still they gazed, and still the wonder grew,
That one small head could carry all he knew.

Oliver Goldsmith

SCHOOLROOM ON A WET AFTERNOON

The unrelated paragraphs of morning
Are forgotten now; the severed heads of kings
Rot by the misty Thames; the roses of York
And Lancaster are pressed between the leaves
of History; negroes sleep in Africa.
The complexities of simple interest lurk
In inkwells and the brittle sticks of chalk:
Afternoon is come and English Grammar.

Rain falls as though the sky has been bereaved,
Stutters its inarticulate grief on glass
Of every lachrymose pane. The children read
Their books or make pretence of concentration,
Each bowed head seems bent on supplication
Or resignation to the fate that waits
In the unmapped forests of the future.
Is it their doomed innocence noon weeps for?

In each diminutive breast a human heart
Pumps out the necessary blood: desires,
Pains and ecstasies surf-ride each singing wave
Which breaks in darkness on the mental shores.
Each child is disciplined; absorbed and still
At his small desk. Yet lift the lid and see,
Amidst frayed books and pencils, other shapes:
Vicious rope, glaring blade, the gun cocked to kill.

                                        Vernon Scannell

Evening Schoolboys

*H*ark to that happy shout! – the school-house door
  Is open thrown, and out the younkers teem;
Some run to leap-frog on the rushy moor,
  And others dabble in the shallow stream,
Catching young fish, and turning pebbles o'er
  For mussel-clams. Look in that mellow gleam,
Where the retiring sun, that rests the while,
  Streams through the broken hedge! How happy seem
Those friendly schoolboys leaning o'er the stile,
  Both reading in one book! – Anon a dream,
Rich with new joys, doth their young hearts beguile,
  And the book's pocketed right hastily.
Ah, happy boys! well may ye turn and smile,
  When joys are yours that never cost a sigh.

John Clare

THE ONE FURROW

When I was young, I went to school
With pencil and foot-rule
Sponge and slate,
And sat on a tall stool
At learning's gate.

When I was older, the gate swung wide;
Clever and keen-eyed
In I pressed,
But found in the mind's pride
No peace, no rest.

Then who was it taught me back to go
To cattle and barrow,
Field and plough;
To keep to the one furrow,
As I do now?

R. S. Thomas

At School-Close

*T*he end has come, as come it must
   To all things; in these sweet June days
The teacher and the scholar trust
   Their parting feet to separate ways.

They part: but in the years to be
   Shall pleasant memories cling to each,
As shells bear inland from the sea
   The murmur of the rhythmic beach . . .

          John Greenleaf Whittier

THE CITY

from PRELUDES

The winter evening settles down
With smell of steaks in passageways.
Six o'clock.
The burnt-out ends of smoky days.
And now a gusty shower wraps
The grimy scraps
Of withered leaves about your feet
And newspapers from vacant lots;
The showers beat
On broken blinds and chimney-pots,
And at the corner of the street
A lonely cab-horse steams and stamps.
And then the lighting of the lamps.

                    T. S. Eliot

LONDON

I wander thro' each charter'd street,
Near where the charter'd Thames does flow,
And mark in every face I meet
Marks of weakness, marks of woe.

In every cry of every Man,
In every Infant's cry of fear,
In every voice, in every ban,
The mind-forg'd manacles I hear.

How the Chimney-sweeper's cry
Every black'ning Church appalls;
And the hapless Soldier's sigh
Runs in blood down Palace walls.

But most thro' midnight streets I hear
How the youthful Harlot's curse
Blasts the new born Infant's tear,
And blights with plagues the Marriage hearse.

William Blake

Suburban Dream

Walking the suburbs in the afternoon
In summer when the idle doors stand open
    And the air flows through the rooms
    Fanning the curtain hems,

You wander through a cool elysium
Of women, schoolgirls, children, garden talks,
    With a schoolboy here and there
    Conning his history book.

The men are all away in offices,
Committee-rooms, laboratories, banks,
    Or pushing cotton goods
    In Wick or Ilfracombe.

The massed unanimous absence liberates
The light keys of the piano and sets free
    Chopin and everlasting youth,
    Now, with the masters gone.

And all things turn to images of peace,
The boy curled over his book, the young girl poised
    On the path as if beguiled
    By the silence of a wood.

It is a child's dream of a grown-up world
But soon the brazen evening clocks will bring
    The tramp of feet and brisk
    Fanfare of motor horns
    And the masters come.

                                        Edwin Muir

Evening: Ponte al Mare, Pisa

The sun is set; the swallows are asleep;
   The bats are flitting fast in the gray air;
The slow soft toads out of damp corners creep,
   And evening's breath, wandering here and there
Over the quivering surface of the stream,
Wakes not one ripple from its summer dream.

There is no dew on the dry grass to-night,
   Nor damp within the shadow of the trees;
The wind is intermitting, dry, and light;
   And in the inconstant motion of the breeze
The dust and straws are driven up and down,
And whirled about the pavement of the town.

Within the surface of the fleeting river
   The wrinkled image of the city lay,
Immovably unquiet, and forever
   It trembles, but it never fades away.

                        Percy Bysshe Shelley

Symphony in Yellow

*A*n omnibus across the bridge
Crawls like a yellow butterfly,
And, here and there, a passer-by
Shows like a little restless midge.

Big barges full of yellow hay
Are moved against the shadowy wharf,
And, like a yellow silken scarf,
The thick fog hangs along the quay.

The yellow leaves begin to fade
And flutter from the Temple elms,
And at my feet the pale green Thames
Lies like a rod of rippled jade.

Oscar Wilde

TOWN OWL

On eves of cold, when slow coal fires,
rooted in basements, burn and branch,
brushing with smoke the city air,

When quartered moons pale in the sky,
and neons glow along the dark
like deadly nightshade on a briar;

Above the muffled traffic then
I hear the owl, and at his note
I shudder in my private chair.

For like an augur he has come
to roost among our crumbling walls,
his blooded talons sheathed in fur.

Some secret lure of time it seems
has called him from his country wastes
to hunt a newer wasteland here.

And where the candelabra swung
bright with the dancers' thousand eyes,
now his black, hooded pupils stare,

And where the silk-shoed lovers ran
with dust of diamonds in their hair,
he opens now his silent wing,

And, like a stroke of doom, drops down,
and swoops across the empty hall,
and plucks a quick mouse off the stair . . .

Laurie Lee

COMPOSED UPON WESTMINSTER BRIDGE, 1802

Earth has not anything to show more fair:
Dull would he be of soul who could pass by
A sight so touching in its majesty:
This City now doth, like a garment, wear
The beauty of the morning; silent, bare,
Ships, towers, domes, theatres, and temples lie
Open unto the fields, and to the sky;
All bright and glittering in the smokeless air
Never did sun more beautifully steep
In his first splendour, valley, rock, or hill;
Ne'er saw I, never felt, a calm so deep!
The river glided at his own sweet will:
Dear God! the very houses seem asleep;
And all that mighty heart is lying still!

William Wordsworth

SNOW IN THE SUBURBS

Every branch big with it,
   Bent every twig with it;
  Every fork like a white web-foot;
  Every street and pavement mute:
Some flakes have lost their way, and grope back upward,
   when
Meeting those meandering down they turn and descend
   again.
    The palings are glued together like a wall,
    And there is no waft of wind with the fleecy fall.

    A sparrow enters the tree,
    Whereon immediately
  A snow-lump thrice his own slight size
Descends on him and showers his head and eyes,
     And overturns him,
     And near inurns him,
  And lights on a nether twig, when its brush
Starts off a volley of other lodging lumps with a rush.

    The steps are a blanched slope,
    Up which, with feeble hope,
  A black cat comes, wide-eyed and thin;
    And we take him in.

Thomas Hardy

Shadwell Stair

I am the ghost of Shadwell Stair.
    Along the wharves by the water-house,
    And through the dripping slaughter-house,
I am the shadow that walks there.

Yet I have flesh both firm and cool,
    And eyes tumultuous as the gems
    Of moons and lamps in the lapping Thames
When dusk sails wavering down the pool.
Shuddering the purple street-arc burns
    Where I watch always; from the banks
    Dolorously the shipping clanks,
And after me a strange tide turns.

I walk till the stars of London wane
    And dawn creeps up the Shadwell Stair.
    But when the crowing sirens blare
I with another ghost am lain.

                                        Wilfred Owen

Leaving Town

*I*t was impossible to leave the town.
Bumping across a maze of obsolete rails
Three times we reached the gasworks and reversed.
We could not get away from the canal;
Dead cats, dead hopes, in those grey deeps immersed,
Over our efforts breathed a spectral prayer.
The cattle-market and the gospel-hall
Returned like fictions of our own despair,
And like Hesperides the suburbs seemed,
Shining far off towards the guiltless fields.
We finished in a little cul-de-sac
Where on the pavement sat a ragged girl
Mourning beside a jug-and-bottle entrance.
Once more we turned the car and started back.

James Reeves

WAR

The Destruction of Sennacherib

The Assyrian came down like the wolf on the fold,
And his cohorts were gleaming in purple and gold;
And the sheen of their spears was like stars on the sea,
When the blue wave rolls nightly on deep Galilee.

Like the leaves of the forest when Summer is green,
That host with their banners, at sunset were seen:
Like the leaves of the forest when Autumn hath blown,
That host on the morrow lay withered and strown.

For the Angel of Death spread his wings on the blast,
And breathed in the face of the foe as he passed;
And the eyes of the sleepers waxed deadly and chill,
And their hearts but once heaved, and for ever grew still!

And there lay the steed with his nostril all wide,
But through it there rolled not the breath of his pride:
And the foam of his gasping lay white on the turf,
And cold as the spray of the rock-beating surf.

And there lay the rider distorted and pale,
With the dew on his brow, and the rust on his mail;
And the tents were all silent, the banners alone,
The lances unlifted, the trumpets unblown.

And the widows of Ashur are loud in their wail,
And the idols are broke in the temple of Baal;
And the might of the Gentile, unsmote by the sword,
Hath melted like snow in the glance of the Lord!

Lord Byron

Harp Song of the Dane Women

What is a woman that you forsake her,
And the hearth-fire and the home-acre,
To go with the old grey Widow-maker?

She has no house to lay a guest in –
But one chill bed for all to rest in,
That the pale suns and the stray bergs nest in.

She has no strong white arms to fold you,
But the ten-times-fingering weed to hold you –
Out on the rocks where the tide has rolled you.

Yet, when the signs of summer thicken,
And the ice breaks, and the birch-buds quicken,
Yearly you turn from our sides, and sicken –

Sicken again for the shouts and the slaughters.
You steal away to the lapping waters,
And look for your ship in her winter-quarters.

You forget our mirth, and talk at the tables,
The kine in the shed and the horse in the stables –
To pitch her sides and go over her cables.

Then you drive out where the storm-clouds swallow,
And the sound of your oar-blades, falling hollow,
Is all we have left through the months to follow.

Ah, what is Woman that you forsake her,
And the hearth-fire and the home-acre
To go with the old grey Widow-maker?

Rudyard Kipling

Bruce's Address before Bannockburn

Scots, wha hae wi' Wallace bled,
Scots, wham Bruce has aften led,
Welcome to your gory bed,
    Or to victorie.

Now's the day, and now's the hour,
See the front o' battle lour!
See approach proud Edward's power –
    Chains and slaverie!

Wha will be a traitor knave?
Wha will fill a coward's grave?
Wha sae base as be a slave?
    Let him turn and flee!

Wha for Scotland's King and law
Freedom's sword will strongly draw,
Freeman stand, or freeman fa'.
    Let him on wi' me!

By oppression's woes and pains!
By your sons in servile chains!
We will drain our dearest veins,
    But they shall be free!

Lay the proud usurpers low!
Tyrants fall in every foe!
Liberty's in every blow!
    Let us do or die!

                            Robert Burns

DRAKE'S DRUM

Drake he's in his hammock an' a thousand mile away,
   (Capten, art tha sleepin' there below?),
Slung atween the round shot in Nombre Dios Bay,
   An' dreamin' arl the time o' Plymouth Hoe.
Yarnder lumes the Island, yarnder lie the ships,
   Wi' sailor-lads a-dancin' heel-an'-toe,
An' the shore-lights flashin', and the night-tide dashin',
   He sees et arl so plainly as he saw et long ago.

Drake he was a Devon man, an' rüled the Devon seas,
   (Capten, art tha sleepin' there below?),
Rovin' tho' his death fell, he went wi' heart at ease,
   An' dreamin' arl the time o' Plymouth Hoe.
'Take my drum to England, hang et by the shore,
   Strike et when your powder's runnin' low;
If the Dons sight Devon, I'll quit the port o' Heaven,
   An' drum them up the channel as we drummed them
   long ago.'

Drake he's in his hammock till the great Armadas come,
   (Capten, art tha sleepin' there below?),
Slung atween the round shot, listenin' for the drum,
   An' dreamin' arl the time o' Plymouth Hoe.
Call him on the deep sea, call him up the Sound,
   Call him when ye sail to meet the foe;
Where the old trade's plyin' an' the old flag flyin'
   They shall find him ware an' wakin', as they found him
   long ago!

                                    Sir Henry Newbolt

AND SHALL TRELAWNY DIE?

A good sword and a trusty hand!
    A merry heart and true!
King James's men shall understand
    What Cornish lads can do.

And have they fixed the where and when?
    And shall Trelawny die?
Here's twenty thousand Cornish men
    Will know the reason why!

Out spake their captain brave and bold,
    A merry wight was he:
'If London Tower were Michael's hold,
    We'll set Trelawny free!

'We'll cross the Tamar, land to land,
    The Severn is no stay, —
With "one and all," and hand in hand,
    And who shall bid us nay?

'And when we come to London Wall,
    A pleasant sight to view,
Come forth! Come forth, ye cowards all,
    Here's men as good as you.
'Trelawny he's in keep and hold
    Trelawny he may die; —
But here's twenty thousand Cornish bold
    Will know the reason why!'

R. S. Hawker

The Charge of the Light Brigade

*H*alf a league, half a league,
Half a league onward,
All in the valley of Death
   Rode the six hundred.
'Forward, the Light Brigade!
Charge for the guns!' he said;
Into the valley of Death
   Rode the six hundred.

'Forward, the Light Brigade!'
Was there a man dismay'd?
Not tho' the soldier knew
   Some one had blunder'd:
Theirs not to make reply,
Theirs not to reason why,
Theirs but to do and die:
Into the valley of Death
   Rode the six hundred.

Cannon to right of them,
Cannon to left of them,
Cannon in front of them
   Volley'd and thunder'd;
Storm'd at with shot and shell,
Boldly they rode and well,
Into the jaws of Death,
Into the mouth of Hell
   Rode the six hundred.

Flash'd all their sabres bare,
Flash'd as they turn'd in air,
Sabring the gunners there,
Charging an army, while
    All the world wonder'd:
Plunged in the battery-smoke
Right thro' the line they broke;
Cossack and Russian
Reel'd from the sabre-stroke
    Shatter'd and sunder'd.
Then they rode back, but not,
    Not the six hundred.

Cannon to right of them,
Cannon to left of them,
Cannon behind them
    Volley'd and thunder'd;
Storm'd at with shot and shell,
While horse and hero fell,
They that had fought so well
Came thro' the jaws of Death
Back from the mouth of Hell,
All that was left of them,
    Left of six hundred.

When can their glory fade?
O the wild charge they made!
    All the world wonder'd.
Honour the charge they made!
Honour the Light Brigade,
    Noble six hundred!

                    Alfred, Lord Tennyson

In Time of 'The Breaking of Nations'

Only a man harrowing clods
   In a slow silent walk
With an old horse that stumbles and nods
   Half asleep as they stalk.

Only thin smoke without flame
   From the heaps of couch-grass;
Yet this will go onward the same
   Though Dynasties pass.

Yonder a maid and her wight
   Come whispering by;
War's annals will cloud into night
   Ere their story die.

Thomas Hardy

THE SECOND WORLD WAR

*T*he voice said 'We are at War'
And I was afraid, for I did not know what this meant.
My sister and I ran to our friends next door
As if they could help. History was lessons learnt
    With ancient dates, but here

    Was something utterly new,
The radio, called the wireless then, had said
That the country would have to be brave. There was
  much to do.
And I remember that night as I lay in bed
    I thought of soldiers who

    Had stood on our nursery floor
Holding guns, on guard and stiff. But war meant blood
Shed over battle-fields, cavalry galloping. War
On that September Sunday made us feel frightened
    Of what our world waited for.

                    Elizabeth Jennings

THE DUG-OUT

Why do you lie with your legs ungainly huddled,
And one arm bent across your sullen, cold,
Exhausted face? It hurts my heart to watch you,
Deep-shadowed from the candle's guttering gold;
And you wonder why I shake you by the shoulder;
Drowsy, you mumble and sigh and turn your head . . .
You are too young to fall asleep for ever;
And when you sleep you remind me of the dead.

Siegfried Sassoon

FUTILITY

Move him into the sun –
Gently its touch awoke him once,
At home, whispering of fields unsown.
Always it woke him, even in France,
Until this morning and this snow.
If anything might rouse him now
The kind old sun will know.

Think how it wakes the seeds, –
Woke, once, the clays of a cold star.
Are limbs, so dear-achieved, are sides,
Full-nerved – still warm – too hard to stir?
Was it for this the clay grew tall?
– O what made fatuous sunbeams toil
To break earth's sleep at all?

Wilfred Owen

O What Is that Sound

O what is that sound which so thrills the ear
   Down in the valley drumming, drumming?
Only the scarlet soldiers, dear,
   The soldiers coming.

O what is that light I see flashing so clear
   Over the distance brightly, brightly?
Only the sun on their weapons, dear,
   As they step lightly.
O what are they doing with all that gear;
   What are they doing this morning, this morning?
Only the usual manoeuvres, dear,
   Or perhaps a warning.

O why have they left the road down there;
   Why are they suddenly wheeling, wheeling?
Perhaps a change in the orders, dear;
   Why are you kneeling?

O haven't they stopped for the doctor's care;
   Haven't they reined their horses, their horses?
Why, they are none of them wounded, dear,
   None of these forces.

O is it the parson they want with white hair;
   Is it the parson, is it, is it?
No, they are passing his gateway, dear,
   Without a visit.

O it must be the farmer who lives so near;
    It must be the farmer so cunning, so cunning;
They have passed the farm already, dear,
    And now they are running.

O where are you going? stay with me here!
    Were the vows you swore me deceiving, deceiving?
No, I promised to love you, dear,
    But I must be leaving.

O it's broken the lock and splintered the door,
    O it's the gate where they're turning, turning;
Their feet are heavy on the floor
    And their eyes are burning.

                                        W. H. Auden

An Irish Airman Foresees His Death

I know that I shall meet my fate
Somewhere among the clouds above;
Those that I fight I do not hate,
Those that I guard I do not love;
My country is Kiltartan Cross,
My countrymen Kiltartan's poor,
No likely end could bring them loss
Or leave them happier than before.
Nor law, nor duty bade me fight,
Nor public men, nor cheering crowds,
A lonely impulse of delight
Drove to this tumult in the clouds;
I balanced all, brought all to mind,
The years to come seemed waste of breath,
A waste of breath the years behind
In balance with this life, this death.

William Butler Yeats

THE SOLDIER

If I should die, think only this of me:
  That there's some corner of a foreign field
That is for ever England. There shall be
  In that rich earth a richer dust concealed;
A dust whom England bore, shaped, made aware,
  Gave, once, her flowers to love, her ways to roam,
A body of England's, breathing English air,
  Washed by the rivers, blest by suns of home.

And think, this heart, all evil shed away,
  A pulse in the eternal mind, no less
    Gives somewhere back the thoughts by England
    given;
Her sights and sounds; dreams happy as her day;
  And laughter, learnt of friends; and gentleness,
    In hearts at peace, under an English heaven.

                                        Rupert Brooke

ANTHEM FOR DOOMED YOUTH

*W*hat passing-bells for these who die as cattle?
Only the monstrous anger of the guns.
Only the stuttering rifles' rapid rattle
Can patter out their hasty orisons.
No mockeries for them; no prayers nor bells,
Nor any voice of mourning save the choirs, –
The shrill, demented choirs of wailing shells;
And bugles calling for them from sad shires.
What candles may be held to speed them all?
Not in the hands of boys, but in their eyes
Shall shine the holy glimmers of good-byes.
The pallor of girls' brows shall be their pall;
Their flowers the tenderness of patient minds,
And each slow dusk a drawing-down of blinds.

                                   Wilfred Owen

MISSING

Less said the better.
The bill unpaid, the dead letter,
No roses at the end
Of Smith, my friend.

Last words don't matter,
And there are none to flatter.
Words will not fill the post
Of Smith, the ghost.

For Smith, our brother,
Only son of loving mother,
The ocean lifted, stirred,
Leaving no word.

John Pudney

IN MEMORIAM (EASTER, 1915)

The flowers left thick at nightfall in the wood
This Eastertide call into mind the men,
Now far from home, who, with their sweethearts, should
Have gathered them and will do never again.

Edward Thomas

REFLECTIONS

It Is Not Growing like a Tree

*I*t is not growing like a tree
   In bulk, doth make man better be:
Or standing long an oak, three hundred year,
To fall a log at last, dry, bald, and sere:
      A lily of a day
      Is fairer far in May,
   Although it fall and die that night;
It was the plant and flower of light.
In small proportions we just beauties see;
And, in short measures, life may perfect be.

Ben Jonson

PAST AND PRESENT

I remember, I remember,
  The house where I was born,
The little window where the sun
  Came peeping in at morn;
He never came a wink too soon
  Nor brought too long a day;
But now, I often wish the night
  Had borne my breath away!

I remember, I remember,
  The roses, red and white,
The violets, and the lily-cups,
  Those flowers made of light!
The lilacs where the robin built,
  And where my brother set
The laburnum on his birth-day, –
  The tree is living yet!

I remember, I remember,
  Where I was used to swing,
And thought the air must rush as fresh
  To swallows on the wing;
My spirit flew in feathers then,
  That is so heavy now,
And summer pools could hardly cool
  The fever on my brow!

I remember, I remember,
    The fir trees dark and high;
I used to think their slender tops
    Were close against the sky:
It was a childish ignorance,
    But now 'tis little joy
To know I'm farther off from Heaven
    Than when I was a boy.

Thomas Hood

JOY

*H*e who binds to himself a joy
Does the wingèd life destroy;
But he who kisses the joy as it flies
Lives in eternity's sun rise.

William Blake

DAFFODILS

I wander'd lonely as a cloud
   That floats on high o'er vales and hills,
When all at once I saw a crowd,
   A host of golden daffodils;
Beside the lake, beneath the trees,
Fluttering and dancing in the breeze.

Continuous as the stars that shine
   And twinkle on the Milky Way,
They stretch'd in never-ending line
   Along the margin of a bay:
Ten thousand saw I at a glance,
Tossing their heads in sprightly dance.

The waves beside them danced, but they
   Out-did the sparkling waves in glee:
A poet could not but be gay,
   In such a jocund company:
I gazed – and gazed – but little thought
What wealth the show to me had brought:

For oft, when on my couch I lie
   In vacant or in pensive mood,
They flash upon that inward eye
   Which is the bliss of solitude;
And then my heart with pleasure fills,
And dances with the daffodils.

William Wordsworth

On Wenlock Edge

On Wenlock Edge the wood's in trouble;
    His forest fleece the Wrekin heaves;
The gale, it plies the saplings double,
    And thick on Severn snow the leaves.

'Twould blow like this through holt and hanger
    When Uricon the city stood:
'Tis the old wind in the old anger,
    But then it threshed another wood.

Then, 'twas before my time, the Roman
    At yonder heaving hill would stare:
The blood that warms an English yeoman,
    The thoughts that hurt him, they were there.

There, like the wind through woods in riot,
    Through him the gale of life blew high;
The tree of man was never quiet:
    Then 'twas the Roman, now 'tis I.

The gale, it plies the saplings double,
    It blows so hard, 'twill soon be gone:
To-day the Roman and his trouble
    Are ashes under Uricon.

                                A. E. Housman

JERUSALEM

*A*nd did those feet in ancient time
   Walk upon England's mountains green?
And was the holy Lamb of God
   On England's pleasant pasture seen?

And did the Countenance Divine
   Shine forth upon our clouded hills?
And was Jerusalem builded here
   Among these dark Satanic Mills?

Bring me my bow of burning gold!
   Bring me my arrows of desire!
Bring me my spear! O clouds, unfold!
   Bring me my chariot of fire!

I will not cease from mental fight,
   Nor shall my sword sleep in my hand,
Till we have built Jerusalem
   In England's green and pleasant land.

                    William Blake

Worldly Hopes

'How sweet is mortal Sovranty!' – think some:
Others – 'How blest the Paradise to come!'
　　Ah, take the Cash in hand and waive the Rest;
Oh, the brave Music of a *distant* Drum! . . .

The Worldly Hope men set their Hearts upon
Turns Ashes – or it prospers; and anon,
　　Like Snow upon the Desert's dusty Face
Lighting a little Hour or two – is gone.

And those who husbanded the Golden Grain,
And those who flung it to the Winds like Rain,
　　Alike to no such aureate Earth are turned
As, buried once, Men want dug up again.

Think, in this battered Caravanserai
Whose Doorways are alternate Night and Day,
　　How Sultan after Sultan with his Pomp
Abode his Hour or two, and went his way.

They say the Lion and the Lizard keep
The Courts where Jamshýd gloried and drank deep;
　　And Bahram, that great Hunter – the Wild Ass
Stamps o'er his Head, and he lies fast asleep.

from The Rubáiyát of Omar Khayyám, translated by
Edward FitzGerald

PREPARATIONS

Yet if His Majesty, our sovereign lord,
Should of his own accord
Friendly himself invite
And say, 'I'll be your guest tomorrow night,'
How should we stir ourselves, call and command
All hands to work! 'Let no man idle stand!
Set me fine Spanish tables in the hall;
See they be fitted all;
Let there be room to eat,
And order taken that there want no meat.
See every sconce and candlestick made bright,
That without tapers they may give a light.
Look to the presence: are the carpets spread,
The dazie o'er head,
The cushions in the chairs,
And all the candles lighted on the stairs?
Perfume the chambers, and in any case
Let each man give attendance in his place!

Thus, if a king were coming, would we do;
And 'twere good reason too;
For 'this a duteous thing
To show all honour to an earthly king,
And after all our travail and our cost,
So he be pleased, to think no labour lost.

But at the coming of the King of Heaven
All's set at six and seven;
We wallow in our sin,
Christ cannot find a chamber in the inn.
We entertain Him always like a stranger,
And, as at first, still lodge Him in the manger.

Anonymous

dazie: canopy over the dais

Things Men Have Made

*T*hings men have made with wakened hands, and put soft
    life into
are awake through years with transferred touch, and go on
    glowing
for long years.
And for this reason, some old things are lovely
warm still with the life of forgotten men who made them.

D. H. Lawrence

THE SELFSAME SONG

A bird sings the selfsame song,
With never a fault in its flow,
That we listened to here those long
    Long years ago.

A pleasing marvel is how
A strain of such rapturous rote
Should have gone on thus till now
    Unchanged in a note!

– But it's not the selfsame bird –
No: perished to dust is he . . .
As also are those who heard
    That song with me.

Thomas Hardy

THIS LIFE

This Life, which seems so fair,
Is like a bubble blown up in the air
    By sporting children's breath,
    Who chase it everywhere,
And strive who can most motion it bequeath.
And though it sometimes seem of its own might
Like to an eye of gold to be fixed there,
And firm to hover in that empty height,
That only is because it is so light.
   But in that pomp it doth not long appear;
For when 'tis most admirèd – in a thought,
Because it erst was nought, it turns to nought.

                William Drummond

I Strove with None

I strove with none, for none was worth my strife;
Nature I loved and, next to Nature, Art:
I warmed both hands before the fire of life;
It sinks, and I am ready to depart.

Walter Savage Landor

SEASONS

THAW

Over the land freckled with snow half-thawed
The speculating rooks at their nests cawed
And saw from elm-tops, delicate as flower of grass,
What we below could not see, Winter pass.

Edward Thomas

THE WINTER IS PAST

For, lo, the winter is past,
The rain is over and gone;
The flowers appear on the earth;
The time of the singing of birds is come,
And the voice of the turtle
  Is heard in our land;
The fig-tree putteth forth her green figs,
And the vines with the tender grape
  Give a good smell.

from The Bible, The Song of Solomon

PIPPA'S SONG

The year's at the spring
And day's at the morn;
Morning's at seven;
The hill-side's dew-pearled;
The lark's on the wing;
The snail's on the thorn:
God's in his heaven –
All's right with the world!

Robert Browning

A CHANGE IN THE YEAR

It is the first mild day of March!
Each minute sweeter than before,
The redbreast sings from the tall larch
That stands beside our door.

There is a blessing in the air,
Which seems a sense of joy to yield
To the bare trees, and mountains bare,
And grass in the green field.

William Wordsworth

To Daffodils

*F*air daffodils, we weep to see
   You haste away so soon:
As yet the early-rising sun
   Has not attained his noon.
      Stay, stay,
    Until the hasting day
      Has run
    But to the even-song;
And, having prayed together, we
    Will go with you along.

We have short time to stay, as you,
   We have as short a spring;
As quick a growth to meet decay,
   As you, or anything.
      We die,
    As your hours do, and dry
      Away,
    Like to the summer's rain;
Or as the pearls of morning's dew
    Ne'er to be found again.

              Robert Herrick

EASTER

I got me flowers to straw Thy way,
I got me boughs off many a tree;
But Thou wast up by break of day,
And brought'st Thy sweets along with Thee.

Yet though my flowers be lost, they say
A heart can never come too late;
Teach it to sing Thy praise this day,
And then this day my life shall date.

George Herbert

Home Thoughts from Abroad

Oh, to be in England
Now that April's there,
And whoever wakes in England
Sees, some morning, unaware,
That the lowest boughs and the brushwood sheaf
Round the elm-tree bole are in tiny leaf,
While the chaffinch sings on the orchard bough
In England – now!
And after April, when May follows,
And the whitethroat builds, and all the swallows!
Hark, where my blossomed pear-tree in the hedge
Leans to the field and scatters on the clover
Blossoms and dewdrops – at the bent spray's edge –
That's the wise thrush; he sings each song twice over,
Lest you should think he never could recapture
The first fine careless rapture!
And though the fields look rough with hoary dew,
All will be gay when noontide wakes anew
The buttercups, the little children's dower
– Far brighter than this gaudy melon-flower.

Robert Browning

Pleasure It Is

Pleasure it is
    To hear, iwis,
   The birdès sing.
The deer in the dale,
The sheep in the vale,
   The corn springing;
God's purveyance
For sustenance
   It is for man.
Then we always
To Him give praise,
   And thank Him than,
   And thank Him than.

William Cornish

iwis: truly

The Lark in the Morning

As I was a-walking
One morning in spring,
I heard a pretty ploughboy,
So sweetly he did sing;
And as he was a-singing
These words I heard him say:
'Oh, there's no life like the ploughboy
All in the month of May.'

There's the lark in the morning
She will rise up from her nest,
She'll mount the white air
With the dew on her breast,
And with the pretty ploughboy O,
She'll whistle and she'll sing,
And at night she'll return
To her nest back again.

Anonymous

SPRING

Nothing is so beautiful as spring –
   When weeds, in wheels, shoot long and lovely and
lush;
   Thrush's eggs look little low heavens, and thrush
Through the echoing timber does so rinse and wring
The ear, it strikes like lightnings to hear him sing;
The glassy pear-tree leaves and blooms, they brush
The descending blue; that blue is all in a rush
With richness; the racing lambs too have fair their fling.

What is all this juice and all this joy?
   A strain of the earth's sweet being in the beginning
In Eden garden. – Have, get, before it cloy,
   Before it cloud, Christ, lord, and sour with sinning,
Innocent mind and Mayday in girl and boy,
   Most, O maid's child, thy choice and worthy the winning.

                    Gerard Manley Hopkins

What Could Be Lovelier than to Hear

*W*hat could be lovelier than to hear
The summer rain
Cutting across the heat, as scythes
Cut across grain?
Falling upon the steaming roof
With sweet uproar,
Tapping and rapping wildly
At the door?

No, do not lift the latch,
But through the pane
We'll stand and watch the circus pageant
Of the rain,
And see the lightning, like a tiger,
Striped and dread,
And hear the thunder cross the sky
With elephant tread.

Elizabeth Coatsworth

THE RAINY SUMMER

There's much afoot in heaven and earth this year;
    The winds hunt up the sun, hunt up the moon,
Trouble the dubious dawn, hasten the drear
    Height of a threatening noon.

No breath of boughs, no breath of leaves, of fronds,
    May linger or grow warm; the trees are loud;
The forest, rooted, tosses in her bonds,
    And strains against the cloud.

No scents may pause within the garden-fold;
    The rifled flowers are cold as ocean-shells;
Bees, humming in the storm, carry their cold
    Wild honey to cold cells.

                                        Alice Meynell

SUMMER

Rushes in a watery place,
    And reeds in a hollow;
A soaring skylark in the sky,
    A darting swallow;
And where pale blossom used to hang
    Ripe fruit to follow.

                            Christina Rossetti

ADLESTROP

Yes. I remember Adlestrop –
The name, because one afternoon
Of heat the express-train drew up there
Unwontedly. It was late June.

The steam hissed. Some one cleared his throat.
No one left and no one came
On the bare platform. What I saw
Was Adlestrop – only the name

And willows, willow-herb, and grass,
And meadowsweet, and haycocks dry,
No whit less still and lonely fair
Than the high cloudlets in the sky.

And for that minute a blackbird sang
Close by, and round him, mistier,
Farther and farther, all the birds
Of Oxfordshire and Gloucestershire.

                                        Edward Thomas

THE THRESHER

Between the upright shafts of those tall elms
We may discern the thresher at his task.
Thump after thump, resounds the constant flail,
That seems to swing uncertain, and yet falls
Full on the destined ear. Wide flies the chaff;
The rustling straw sends up a frequent mist
Of atoms, sparkling in the noon-day beam.

from 'The Task', William Cowper

MOONLIGHT, SUMMER MOONLIGHT

'Tis moonlight, summer moonlight,
    All soft and still and fair;
The silent time of midnight
    Shines sweetly everywhere,

But most where trees are sending
    Their breezy boughs on high,
Or stooping low are lending
    A shelter from the sky.

Emily Brontë

from SUMMER IMAGES

I love the south-west wind, or low or loud,
  And not the less when sudden drops of rain
Moisten my pallid cheek from ebon cloud,
  Threatening soft showers again,
That over lands new ploughed and meadow grounds,
  Summer's sweet breath unchain,
   And wake harmonious sounds.

Rich music breathes in summer's every sound;
  And in her harmony of varied greens,
Woods, meadows, hedge-rows, corn-fields, all around
  Much beauty intervenes,
Filling with harmony the ear and eye;
  While o'er the mingling scenes
   Far spreads the laughing sky.

John Clare

Autumn Song

*T*here came a day that caught the summer
Wrung its neck
Plucked it
And ate it.

Now what shall I do with the trees?
The day said, the day said.
Strip them bare, strip them bare.
Let's see what is really there.

And what shall I do with the sun?
The day said, the day said.
Roll him away till he's cold and small.
He'll come back rested if he comes back at all.

And what shall I do with the birds?
The day said, the day said.
The birds I've frightened, let them flit,
I'll hang out pork for the brave tomtit.

And what shall I do with the seed?
The day said, the day said.
Bury it deep, see what it's worth.
See if it can stand the earth.

What shall I do with the people?
The day said, the day said.
Stuff them with apple and blackberry pie –
They'll love me then till the day they die.

There came this day and he was autumn.
His mouth was wide
And red as a sunset.
His tail was an icicle.

Ted Hughes

SOMETHING TOLD THE WILD GEESE

Something told the wild geese
It was time to go,
Though the fields lay golden
Something whispered, 'Snow!'
Leaves were green and stirring,
Berries lustre-glossed,
But beneath warm feathers
Something cautioned, 'Frost!'

All the sagging orchards
Steamed with amber spice,
But each wild beast stiffened
At remembered ice.
Something told the wild geese
It was time to fly –
Summer sun was on their wings,
Winter in their cry.

Rachel Field

November Night

*L*isten . . .
With faint dry sound,
Like steps of passing ghosts,
The leaves, frost-crisped, break from the trees
And fall.

Adelaide Crapsey

Fall, Leaves, Fall

*F*all, leaves, fall; die, flowers, away;
Lengthen night and shorten day;
Every leaf speaks bliss to me
Fluttering from the autumn tree.

I shall smile when wreaths of snow
Blossom where the rose should grow;
I shall sing when night's decay
Ushers in a drearier day.

Emily Brontë

Autumn

I love the fitful gust that shakes
  The casement all the day,
And from the glossy elm tree takes
  The faded leaves away,
Twirling them by the window pane
With thousand others down the lane.

I love to see the shaking twig
  Dance till shut of eve,
The sparrow on the cottage rig,
  Whose chirp would make believe
That spring was just now flirting by
In Summer's lap with flowers to lie.

I love to see the cottage smoke
  Curl upwards through the trees;
The pigeons nestled round the cote
  On November days like these;
The cock upon the dunghill crowing,
The mill sails on the heath a-going.

      John Clare

from A SHEEP FAIR

The day arrives of the autumn fair,
    And torrents fall,
Though sheep in throngs are gathered there,
    Ten thousand all,
Sodden, with hurdles round them reared:
And, lot by lot, the pens are cleared,
And the auctioneer wrings out his beard,
And wipes his book, bedrenched and smeared,
And rakes the rain from his face with the edge of his
   hand,
    As torrents fall.

Thomas Hardy

NOVEMBER

*T*he sheep, before the pinching heaven,
To sheltered dale and down are driven,
Where yet some faded herbage pines,
And yet a watery sunbeam shines:
In meek despondency they eye
The withered sward and wintry sky,
And far beneath their summer hill
Stray sadly by Glenkinnon's rill:
The shepherd shifts his mantle's fold,
And wraps him closer from the cold;
His dogs no merry circles wheel,
But, shivering, follow at his heel;
A cowering glance they often cast,
As deeper moans the gathering blast.

from Marmion, Sir Walter Scott

Autumn: A Dirge

The warm sun is failing, the bleak wind is wailing,
The bare boughs are sighing, the pale flowers are dying;
        And the Year
On the earth her death-bed, in a shroud of leaves dead,
        Is lying.
    Come, Months, come away,
    From November to May,
    In your saddest array;
    Follow the bier
    Of the dead cold Year,
And like dim shadows watch by her sepulchre.

The chill rain is falling, the nipped worm is crawling,
The rivers are swelling, the thunder is knelling
        For the Year;
The blithe swallows are flown, and the lizards each gone
        To his dwelling.
    Come, Months, come away;
    Put on white, black, and grey;
    Let your light sisters play –
    Ye, follow the bier
    Of the dead cold Year,
And make her grave green with tear on tear.

                                    Percy Bysshe Shelley

No!

No sun – no moon!
  No morn – no noon –
No dawn – no dusk – no proper time of day –
  No sky – no earthly view –
  No distance looking blue –
No road – no street – no 't'other side the way' –
  No end to any Row –
  No indications where the Crescents go –
  No top to any steeple –
No recognitions of familiar people –
  No courtesies for showing 'em –
  No knowing 'em! –
No travelling at all – no locomotion,
No inkling of the way – no notion –
  'No go' – by land or ocean –
  No mail – no post –
No news from any foreign coast –
No Park – no Ring – no afternoon gentility –
  No company – no nobility –
No warmth, no cheerfulness, no healthful ease,
No comfortable feel in any member –
No shade, no shine, no butterflies, no bees,
No fruits, no flowers, no leaves, no birds –
  November!

Thomas Hood

WINTER THE HUNTSMAN

*T*hrough his iron glades
Rides Winter the Huntsman,
All colour fades
As his horn is heard sighing.

Far through the forest
His wild hooves crash and thunder
Till many a mighty branch
Is torn asunder.

And the red reynard creeps
To his hole near the river,
The copper leaves fall
And the bare trees shiver.

As night creeps from the ground,
Hides each tree from its brother,
And each dying sound
Reveals yet another.

Is it Winter the Huntsman
Who gallops through his iron glades,
Cracking his cruel whip
To the gathering shades?

                                        Osbert Sitwell

WINTER SHOOT

*S*ee! from the brake the whirring pheasant springs,
And mounts exulting on triumphant wings;
Short in his joy, he feels the fiery wound,
Flutters in blood, and panting beats the ground.
Ah! what avail his glossy, varying dyes,
His purple crest, and scarlet-circled eyes,
The vivid green his shining plumes unfold,
His painted wings, and breast that flames with gold?

With slaughtering guns the unwearied fowler roves,
When frosts have whitened all the naked groves;
Where doves in flocks the leafless trees o'ershade,
And lonely woodcocks haunt the watery glade.
He lifts the tube, and levels with his eye:
Straight a short thunder breaks the frozen sky.
Oft, as in airy rings they skim the heath,
The clamorous lapwings feel the leaden death:
Oft, as the mounting larks their notes prepare,
They fall, and leave their little lives in air.

from Windsor Forest, Alexander Pope

STOPPING BY WOODS ON A SNOWY EVENING

Whose woods these are I think I know.
His house is in the village though;
He will not see me stopping here
To watch his woods fill up with snow.

My little horse must think it queer
To stop without a farmhouse near
Between the woods and frozen lake
The darkest evening of the year.

He gives his harness bells a shake
To ask if there is some mistake.
The only other sound's the sweep
Of easy wind and downy flake.

The woods are lovely, dark and deep,
But I have promises to keep,
And miles to go before I sleep,
And miles to go before I sleep.

Robert Frost

Song

A widow bird sate mourning for her love
   Upon a wintry bough;
The frozen wind crept on above,
   The freezing stream below.

There was no leaf upon the forest bare,
   No flower upon the ground,
And little motion in the air
   Except the mill-wheel's sound.

Percy Bysshe Shelley

In a Drear-Nighted December

In a drear-nighted December,
   Too happy, happy tree,
Thy branches ne'er remember
   Their green felicity:
The north cannot undo them
With a sleety whistle through them;
Nor frozen thawings glue them
    From budding at the prime.

In a drear-nighted December,
   Too happy, happy brook,
Thy bubblings ne'er remember
   Apollo's summer look;
But with a sweet forgetting,
They stay their crystal fretting,
Never, never petting
    About the frozen time.

Ah! would 'twere so with many
   A gentle girl and boy!
But were there ever any
   Writhed not at passèd joy?
To know the change and feel it,
When there is none to heal it
Nor numbèd sense to steal it,
    Was never said in rhyme.

John Keats

When Icicles Hang by the Wall

*W*hen icicles hang by the wall,
  And Dick the shepherd blows his nail;
When Tom bears logs into the hall,
  And milk comes frozen home in pail;
When blood is nipped, and ways be foul,
– Then nightly sings the staring owl:
  To-who,
To-whit, *To-who* – a merry note,
While greasy Joan doth keel the pot.

When all aloud the wind doth blow,
  And coughing drowns the parson's saw,
And birds sit brooding in the snow,
  And Marian's nose looks red and raw;
When roasted crabs hiss in the bowl,
– Then nightly sings the staring owl:
  To-who,
To-whit, *To-who* – a merry note,
While greasy Joan doth keel the pot.

from Love's Labour's Lost, William Shakespeare

keel: skim
crabs: crab-apples

SKATING

And in the frosty season, when the sun
Was set, and visible for many a mile
The cottage windows blazed through twilight gloom,
I heeded not their summons: happy time
It was indeed for all of us – for me
It was a time of rapture. Clear and loud
The village clock tolled six, – I wheeled about,
Proud and exulting like an untired horse
That cares not for his home. All shod with steel,
We hissed along the polished ice in games
Confederate, imitative of the chase
And woodland pleasures, – the resounding horn,
The pack loud chiming, and the hunted hare.
So through the darkness and the cold we flew,
And not a voice was idle; with the din
Smitten, the precipices rang aloud;
The leafless trees and every icy crag
Tinkled like iron; while far-distant hills
Into the tumult sent an alien sound
Of melancholy not unnoticed, while the stars
Eastward were sparkling clear, and in the west
The orange sky of evening died away.

                              William Wordsworth

DEATH OF A SNOWMAN

I was awake all night,
Big as a polar bear,
Strong and firm and white.
The tall black hat I wear
Was draped with ermine fur.
I felt so fit and well
Till the world began to stir
And the morning sun swell.
I was tired, began to yawn;
At noon in the humming sun
I caught a severe warm;
My nose began to run.
My hat grew black and fell,
Was followed by my grey head.
There was no funeral bell,
But by tea-time I was dead.

Vernon Scannell

A CHILD'S VOICE

On winter nights shepherd and I
   Down to the lambing shed would go;
Rain round our swinging lamp did fly
   Like shining flakes of snow.

There on a nail our lamp we hung,
   And O it was beyond belief
To see those ewes lick with hot tongues
   The limp wet lambs to life.

A week gone and sun shining warm
   It was as good as gold to hear
Those new-born voices round the farm
   Cry shivering and clear.

Where was a prouder man than I
   Who knew the night those lambs were born
Watching them leap two feet on high
   And stamp the ground in scorn?

Gone sheep and shed and lighted rain
   And blue March morning; yet today
A small voice crying brings again
   Those lambs leaping at play.

Andrew Young

Journey's End

Up-Hill

*D*oes the road wind up-hill all the way?
    Yes, to the very end.
Will the day's journey take the whole long day?
    From morn to night, my friend.

But is there for the night a resting-place?
    A roof for when the slow dark hours begin.
May not the darkness hide it from my face?
    You cannot miss that inn.

Shall I meet other wayfarers at night?
    Those who have gone before.
Then must I knock, or call when just in sight?
    They will not keep you standing at that door.

Shall I find comfort, travel-sore and weak?
    Of labour you shall find the sum.
Will there be beds for me and all who seek?
    Yea, beds for all who come.

Christina Rossetti

IN TIME OF PESTILENCE
1593

*A*dieu, farewell earth's bliss!
This world uncertain is:
Fond are life's lustful joys,
Death proves them all but toys.
None from his darts can fly;
I am sick, I must die –
   Lord, have mercy upon us!

Rich men, trust not in wealth,
Gold cannot buy you health;
Physic himself must fade;
All things to end are made;
The plague full swift goes by;
I am sick, I must die –
   Lord, have mercy upon us!

Beauty is but a flower
Which wrinkles will devour;
Brightness falls from the air;
Queens have died young and fair;
Dust hath closed Helen's eye;
I am sick, I must die –
   Lord, have mercy upon us!

Strength stoops unto the grave,
Worms feed on Hector brave;
Swords may not fight with fate;
Earth still holds ope her gate;
Come, come! the bells do cry;
I am sick, I must die –
   Lord, have mercy upon us!

Wit with his wantonness
Tasteth death's bitterness;
Hell's executioner
Hath no ears for to hear
What vain art can reply;
I am sick, I must die –
   Lord, have mercy upon us!

Haste therefore each degree
To welcome destiny;
Heaven is our heritage,
Earth's but a player's stage.
Mount·we unto the sky;
I am sick, I must die –
   Lord, have mercy upon us!

Thomas Nashe

from ELEGY WRITTEN IN A COUNTRY
CHURCHYARD

The curfew tolls the knell of parting day,
The lowing herd wind slowly o'er the lea,
The ploughman homeward plods his weary way,
And leaves the world to darkness and to me.

Now fades the glimmering landscape on the sight,
And all the air a solemn stillness holds,
Save where the beetle wheels his droning flight,
And drowsy tinklings lull the distant folds.

Save that from yonder ivy-mantled tow'r
The moping owl does to the moon complain
Of such as, wandering near her secret bow'r,
Molest her ancient solitary reign.

Beneath those rugged elms, that yew-tree's shade,
Where heaves the turf in many a mould'ring heap,
Each in his narrow cell for ever laid,
The rude forefathers of the hamlet sleep.

The breezy call of incense-breathing morn,
The swallow twitt'ring from the straw-built shed,
The cock's shrill clarion or the echoing horn,
No more shall rouse them from their lowly bed.

For them no more the blazing hearth shall burn,
Or busy housewife ply her evening care:
No children run to lisp their sire's return,
Or climb his knees the envied kiss to share.

Oft did the harvest to their sickle yield,
Their furrow oft the stubborn glebe has broke;
How jocund did they drive their team afield!
How bow'd the woods beneath their sturdy stroke!

Let not Ambition mock their useful toil,
Their homely joys and destiny obscure;
Nor Grandeur hear, with a disdainful smile,
The short and simple annals of the poor.

The boast of heraldry, the pomp of pow'r,
And all that beauty, all that wealth e'er gave,
Awaits alike th' inevitable hour.
The paths of glory lead but to the grave.

                                        Thomas Gray

FIDELE

*F*ear no more the heat o' the sun
   Nor the furious winter's rages;
Thou thy worldly task hast done,
   Home art gone and ta'en thy wages:
Golden lads and girls all must,
As chimney-sweepers, come to dust.

Fear no more the frown o' the great,
   Thou art past the tyrant's stroke;
Care no more to clothe and eat;
   To thee the reed is as the oak:
The sceptre, learning, physic, must
All follow this, and come to dust.

Fear no more the lightning-flash
   Nor the all-dreaded thunder-stone
Fear not slander, censure rash;
   Thou hast finish'd joy and moan:
All lovers young, all lovers must
Consign to thee, and come to dust.

from Cymbeline, William Shakespeare

Because I Could Not Stop for Death

Because I could not stop for Death –
He kindly stopped for me –
The Carriage held but just Ourselves –
And Immortality.

We slowly drove – He knew no haste
And I had put away
My labor and my leisure too,
For His Civility –

We passed the School, where Children strove
At Recess – in the Ring –
We passed the Fields of Gazing Grain –
We passed the Setting Sun –

Or rather – He passed Us –
The Dews drew quivering and chill –
For only Gossamer, my Gown –
My Tippet – only Tulle –

We paused before a House that seemed
A Swelling of the Ground –
The Roof was scarcely visible –
The Cornice – in the Ground –

Since then – 'tis Centuries – and yet
Feels shorter than the Day
I first surmised the Horses' Heads
Were toward Eternity –

                                        Emily Dickinson

A Slumber Did My Spirit Seal

A slumber did my spirit seal;
   I had no human fears:
She seem'd a thing that could not feel
   The touch of earthly years.

No motion has she now, no force;
   She neither hears nor sees;
Roll'd round in earth's diurnal course
   With rocks, and stones, and trees.

William Wordsworth

Fare Well

*W*hen I lie where shades of darkness
Shall no more assail mine eyes,
Nor the rain make lamentation
   When the wind sighs;
How will fare the world whose wonder
Was the very proof of me?
Memory fades, must the remembered
   Perishing be?

Oh, when this my dust surrenders
Hand, foot, lip, to dust again,
May these loved and loving faces
    Please other men!
May the rusting harvest hedgerow
Still the Traveller's Joy entwine,
And as happy children gather
    Posies once mine.

Look thy last on all things lovely,
Every hour. Let no night
Seal thy sense in deathly slumber
    Till to delight
Thou have paid thy utmost blessing;
Since that all things thou wouldst praise
Beauty took from those who loved them
    In other days.

Walter de la Mare

FUNERAL BLUES

Stop all the clocks, cut off the telephone,
Prevent the dog from barking with a juicy bone,
Silence the pianos and with muffled drum
Bring out the coffin, let the mourners come.
Let aeroplanes circle moaning overhead
Scribbling on the sky the message He is Dead.
Put crêpe bows round the white necks of the public doves,
Let the traffic policemen wear black cotton gloves.

He was my North, my South, my East and West,
My working week and my Sunday rest,
My noon, my midnight, my talk, my song;
I thought that love would last for ever: I was wrong.

The stars are not wanted now: put out every one,
Pack up the moon and dismantle the sun,
Pour away the ocean and sweep up the wood;
For nothing now can ever come to any good.

W. H. Auden

Requiem

Under the wide and starry sky
  Dig the grave and let me lie:
Glad did I live and gladly die,
  And I laid me down with a will.

This be the verse you grave for me:
Here he lies where he long'd to be;
Home is the sailor, home from sea,
  And the hunter home from the hill.

Robert Louis Stevenson

Cities and Thrones and Powers

Cities and Thrones and Powers,
　　Stand in Time's eye,
Almost as long as flowers,
　　Which daily die:
But, as new buds put forth
　　To glad new men,
Out of the spent and unconsidered Earth,
　　The Cities rise again.

This season's Daffodil,
　　She never hears
What change, what chance, what chill,
　　Cut down last year's;
But with bold countenance,
　　And knowledge small,
Esteems her seven days' continuance,
　　To be perpetual.

So Time that is o'er-kind
　　To all that be,
Ordains us e'en as blind,
　　As bold as she:
That in our very death,
　　And burial sure,
Shadow to shadow, well persuaded, saith,
　　'See how our works endure!'

                              Rudyard Kipling

And Death Shall Have No Dominion

And death shall have no dominion.
Dead men naked they shall be one
With the man in the wind and the west moon;
When their bones are picked clean and the clean bones gone,
They shall have stars at elbow and foot;
Though they go mad they shall be sane,
Though they sink through the sea they shall rise again;
Though lovers be lost love shall not;
And death shall have no dominion.

And death shall have no dominion.
Under the windings of the sea
They lying long shall not die windily;
Twisting on racks when sinews give way,
Strapped to a wheel, yet they shall not break;
Faith in their hands shall snap in two,
And the unicorn evils run them through;
Split all ends up they shan't crack;
And death shall have no dominion.

And death shall have no dominion.
No more may gulls cry at their ears
Or waves break loud on the seashores;
Where blew a flower may a flower no more
Lift its head to the blows of the rain;
Though they be mad and dead as nails,
Heads of the characters hammer through daisies;
Break in the sun till the sun breaks down,
And death shall have no dominion.

                                        Dylan Thomas

INDEX OF POETS

INDEX OF POEMS

INDEX OF FIRST LINES

ACKNOWLEDGEMENTS

The editor and publishers gratefully acknowledge permission to reproduce copyright material in this book:

'O What Is that Sound' and 'Funeral Blues' by W. H. Auden from *Collected Poems* by W. H. Auden, edited by Edward Mendelson by permission of Faber & Faber Ltd; 'O Child Beside the Waterfall' by George Barker reprinted from *To Aylsham Fair* and 'To My Mother' by George Barker reprinted from *Collected Poems*, both by permission of Faber & Faber Ltd; 'Tarantella', 'Henry King' and 'Matilda' by Hilaire Belloc reprinted from *The Complete Verse of Hilaire Belloc* by permission of Peters Fraser & Dunlop Group Ltd; 'Thames Gulls' by Edmund Blunden reprinted from *The Poems of Edmund Blunden 1914-1930* by permission of Peters Fraser & Dunlop Group Ltd; 'Colonel Fazackerley' and 'My Mother Saw a Dancing Bear' by Charles Causley reprinted from *Figgie Hobbin* (Macmillan, London & Basingstoke) and 'Timothy Winters' by Charles Causley reprinted from *Collected Poems* (Macmillan, London & Basingstoke) all by permission of David Higham Associates Ltd; 'What Could Be Lovelier than to Hear' by Elizabeth Coatsworth from *Poems* © 1940 by Macmillan Publishing Company, renewed 1968 by Elizabeth Coatsworth Beston; 'Childhood' and 'Night Song' by Frances Cornford reprinted from *Collected Poems* (Hutchinson) by permission of Random House UK Ltd; 'The Listeners', 'Echo' and 'Fare Well' by Walter de la Mare reprinted from *The Complete Poems of Walter de la Mare* by permission of The Literary Trustees of Walter de la Mare and The Society of Authors as their representative; extract from 'Preludes' by T. S. Eliot reprinted from *Collected Poems 1909-1962* and 'Macavity' by T. S. Eliot reprinted from *Old Possum's Book of Practical Cats* both by permission of Faber & Faber Ltd; 'The Road Not Taken', 'The Runaway' and 'Stopping by Woods on a Snowy Evening' by Robert Frost reprinted from *The Poetry of Robert Frost* edited by Edward Connery Latham (Jonathan Cape) by permission of Random House (UK) Ltd and the Estate of Robert Frost; 'She Tells her Love While Half Asleep' by Robert Graves reprinted from *Collected Poems 1975* by permission of A. P. Watt Ltd on behalf of the Trustees of Robert Graves Copyright Trust; 'Considering the Snail' by Thom Gunn reprinted from *My Sad Captains* by permission of Faber & Faber Ltd; 'Sally' by Phoebe Hesketh reprinted from *Song of Sunlight* (The Bodley Head) by permission of Random House (UK) Ltd; 'My Sister Jane' by Ted Hughes reprinted from *Meet My Folks!* and 'Autumn Song' by Ted Hughes reprinted from *Season Songs* both by permission of Faber and Faber Ltd; 'My Grandmother' reprinted from *Collected Poems* and 'The Second World War' by Elizabeth Jennings, by permission of David Higham Associates Ltd; 'Days' and 'Take One Home for the Kiddies' by Philip Larkin reprinted from *The Whitsun Weddings*, 'The Explosion' by Philip Larkin reprinted from *High Windows*, all by permission of Faber and Faber Ltd; 'Town Owl' by Laurie Lee reprinted from *Selected Poems* reprinted by permission of Peters Fraser and Dunlop Group Ltd; 'Sea Fever' reprinted from *Salt Water Ballads* by John Masefield by permission of The Society of Authors; 'Suburban Dream' by Edwin Muir reprinted from *Collected Poems* by permission of Faber and Faber Ltd; 'The Termite' © 1942 by Ogden Nash, renewed, reprinted from *Verses from 1929 On* (Little, Brown) by permission of Curtis Brown Ltd; 'The Moon Is Up' by Alfred Noyes reprinted from *Collected Poems* by permission of the Executors of Alfred Noyes Literary Estate; 'Street Boy' by Gareth Owen reprinted from *Young Winter's Tales, 5* (Macmillan London Ltd, 1974) by permission of the author c/o Rogers, Coleridge & White Ltd; 'One Perfect Rose' by Dorothy Parker reprinted from *The Collected Dorothy Parker* (first published 1944) by permission of Gerald Duckworth & Co. Ltd; 'A Small Dragon' by Brian Patten reprinted from *Notes to the Hurrying Man* (George, Allen and Unwin) by permission of HarperCollins Publishers Ltd; 'Pheasant' by Sylvia Plath from *Crossing the Water* by permission of Faber and Faber Ltd, 'Morning Song' reprinted from *Ariel* by Sylvia Plath by permission of Faber and Faber Ltd; 'The Ghoul' by Jack Prelutsky reprinted from *Nightmares, Poems to Trouble Your Sleep* by Jack Prelutsky by permission of A & C Black (Publishers) Ltd; 'Missing' by John Pudney reprinted from *Beyond This Disregard* by permission of David Higham Associates Ltd; 'Leaving Town' © James Reeves reprinted from *Collected Poems 1929-1974* (Heinemann) and 'The Snitterjipe' © James Reeves from *Complete Poems for Children* (Heinemann) by permission of The James Reeves Estate and Laura Cecil Literary Agency as their representative; 'Sir Smasham Uppe' by E. V. Rieu from *Cuckoo Calling* (Methuen 1933) by permission of Richard Rieu; 'My Papa's Waltz' by Theodore Roethke reprinted from *Collected Poems* by permission of Faber & Faber Ltd; 'Everyone Sang' © 1920 (E. P. Dutton) copyright renewed 1948 by Siegfried Sassoon, 'Middle Ages' © 1918, 1920 (E. P. Dutton), copyright 1936, 1946, 1947, 1948 by Siegfried Sassoon, and 'The Dug-out' © 1918, 1920 (E. P. Dutton), copyright 1936, 1946, 1947, 1948 by

Siegfried Sassoon, from *Collected Poems of Siegfried Sassoon* by permission of Viking Penguin, a division of Penguin Books USA Inc.; 'Death of a Snowman' by Vernon Scannell reprinted from *The Apple-Raid and Other Poems* (Chatto 1974) and 'Schoolroom on a Wet Afternoon' by Vernon Scannell reprinted from *A Mortal Pitch* (Villiers Publications 1957) by permission of the author; 'The Visitor' by Ian Serraillier reprinted from *A Second Poetry Book* edited by John Foster (Oxford University Press 1980) by permission of the author; 'Ghosts' © 1957 by Robert Service by permission of The Estate of Robert Service; 'Winter the Huntsman' by Osbert Sitwell © Mr Frank Magro reprinted from *Selected Poems Old and New* (Duckworth) by permission of David Higham Associates Ltd; 'The Singing Cat' by Stevie Smith from *The Collected Poems of Stevie Smith* (Penguin 20th Century Classics) by permission of James MacGibbon; 'My Parents Kept Me from Children who Were Rough' by Stephen Spender from *Collected Poems 1928–1985* by permission of Faber and Faber Ltd; 'The Rivals' by James Stephens by permission of The Society of Authors on behalf of the copyright owner, Mrs Iris Wise; 'And Death Shall Have No Dominion' by Dylan Thomas reprinted from *Collected Poems* (J. M. Dent) by permission of David Higham Associates Ltd; 'A Child's Voice' by Andrew Young reprinted from *The Poetical Works of Andrew Young* edited by Edward Lowbury & Alison Young (Secker & Warburg, 1985) by permission of The Andrew Young Estate.

Every effort has been made to trace copyright holders. The editor and publishers would like to hear from any copyright holders not acknowledged.